M000249086

ONCE A PROFESSOR

Once a Professor

A Memoir of Teaching
in Turbulent Times

JERRY APPS

Wisconsin Historical Society Press

Published by the Wisconsin Historical Society Press
Publishers since 1855

The Wisconsin Historical Society helps people connect to the past by collecting, preserving, and sharing stories. Founded in 1846, the Society is one of the nation's finest historical institutions.
Join the Wisconsin Historical Society: wisconsinhistory.org/membership

All photos are from the author's collection unless otherwise credited.
Photographs identified with WHI or WHS are from the Society's collections; address requests to reproduce these photos to the Visual Materials Archivist at the Wisconsin Historical Society, 816 State Street, Madison, WI 53706.

Printed in Canada
Designed by Diana Boger
22 21 20 19 18   1 2 3 4 5

Library of Congress Cataloging-in-Publication Data
Names: Apps, Jerold W., 1934– author.
Title: Once a professor : a memoir of teaching in turbulent times / Jerry Apps.
Description: Madison, Wisconsin : Wisconsin Historical Society Press, [2018] |
    Includes bibliographical references. |
Identifiers: LCCN 2017037407 (print) | LCCN 2017044974 (e-book) |
    ISBN 9780870208584 (E-book) | ISBN 9780870208577 (Hardcover : alk. paper)
Subjects: LCSH: Apps, Jerold W., 1934– | College teachers—United States—Biography. |
    University of Wisconsin—Madison—History.
Classification: LCC LA2317.A63 (e-book) | LCC LA2317.A63 A3 2018 (print) |
    DDC 378.12092 [B] —dc23
LC record available at https://lccn.loc.gov/2017037407

♾ The paper used in this publication meets the minimum requirements of the American National Standard for Information Sciences—Permanence of Paper for Printed Library Materials, ANSI Z39.48–1992.

For Professor Walter Bjoraker,
my undergraduate advisor

Courtesy of the UW–Madison Archives, #S10345

Contents

Preface

I never wanted to be a college professor. As a kid growing up on a farm, I had met only one professor, a slow-talking old man who taught at a small Ohio college and spent his summers on the family farm near Wild Rose. He didn't say much, and when he did speak I usually couldn't understand what he said. The people around Wild Rose found him odd. To me he seemed a little strange—and a lot boring.

When I was in grade school, I thought it might be fun to teach in a one-room country school like the one I attended. Then, after I was struck with polio during the winter I was in eighth grade, I began reading everything I could get my hands on—novels, history, biographies, poetry. I would never play high school sports or participate in vigorous physical activities like the other kids in my class, so instead I studied a lot, edited the high school newspaper, and entered speaking contests. I even learned to enjoy public speaking (thanks to my time announcing basketball games at Wild Rose High School), and I thought I might want to teach high school agriculture one day. Still, the idea of being a professor never crossed my mind.

Here I am as a sixteen-year-old high school graduate, about to leave home for Madison.

• • •

I enrolled at the University of Wisconsin–Madison in the College of Agriculture for the fall semester of 1951 as a new freshman. I had just turned seventeen. I was alone in the big city, and I was scared to death. I had never lived in a city, and I knew no one. I liked the quiet of the country, the country smells and sounds, and the feelings that went along with country life.

I had graduated from Wild Rose High School that spring at the age of sixteen. To my great surprise, as valedictorian of my class I had earned a tuition scholarship to attend the state's big university (as people referred to it in those days). My scholarship was worth $63.50, which, as my dad said, was a lot of money. Times were tough on the home farm during the early 1950s, and I had given little thought to attending college. Without the scholarship I never would have been able to go.

Along with carrying a full-time class load, I worked forty hours a week so I could earn enough money to cover my expenses. I rented a room for five dollars a week, cooked most of my meals there, and studied. I had little time or money for social activities other than study groups. To those interested in college social life, I must have appeared to be the most boring guy they'd ever met.

But I was enjoying every minute of it. I was awash in new ideas that challenged me to think about things I had never thought about. I liked getting to know my professors, who had vocabularies that far exceeded mine and ideas I had never considered.

The Korean Conflict had begun in 1950, and at the UW I enrolled in the Reserve Officers Training Corps, a requirement for all male freshmen. No army doctor ever asked me if I had had polio, and I didn't volunteer xii • ONCE A PROFESSOR

the information. I suspect I could have gotten a medical deferment, but I didn't want one. Neverthless, ROTC duty provided a deferment from the draft. It also provided ample opportunities for marching, which helped strengthen my weak leg.

After four years in ROTC, I received a commission as a second lieutenant in the US Army Reserve and was expected to go on active duty for two years upon graduation in 1955. By then I had earned a teaching certificate, which would allow me to teach vocational agriculture and biology in any Wisconsin high school. But army service came first.

While serving on active duty in the military at Fort Eustis, Virginia, I had little to do, as the hostilities in Korea had ceased in 1953. I was assigned to the 507th Transportation Battalion, moving people from here to there. When I had finished my day's assignment, I drank coffee at the PX, chatted with my fellow second lieutenants, and did a lot of thinking about my future plans. I decided that teaching in a high school classroom wasn't really what I wanted to do. I had practice-taught at five high schools while earning my teaching certificate, and to me the work seemed too confining, too caught up in rules and regulations.

I thought about working in a business related to agriculture, maybe for a feed or implement company. They were always looking for college graduates with farm backgrounds. I also considered returning to the home farm, where I knew my parents could use my help. My two-year army obligation was down to six months, with six years of reserve duty to follow, and the army had more second lieutenants than it needed. So what would I do next?

In the summer of 1956, when I was released from active military duty, I stopped in Madison to see my undergraduate advisor, Professor Walter Bjoraker, chair of UW–Madison's Department of Agricultural and Extension Education. We chatted for a time, and then, out of the blue, Professor Bjoraker asked me, "Would you be interested in working on a master's degree?"

Graduate work was something I had never considered. "Maybe," I replied. Working on my master's would give me a year to make up my mind about my career options.

"We've just hired a new assistant professor, George Sledge. Would you like to be his research assistant?"

"Tell me more," I said.

Professor Bjoraker described the research project, which included doing a survey of the vocational aspirations of high school graduates from predominately rural communities. He told me I would receive a monthly income for working half-time for Professor Sledge. He also said I could use the research findings from the project for my master's thesis. It was an offer I couldn't pass up.

I enrolled in the graduate program in the fall of 1956, signing up for courses in animal science, agronomy, and Introduction to Extension. That last one really caught my attention. I had been a 4-H member for ten years, and I knew Henry Haferbecker, the county extension agent back home in Waushara County. I knew a bit about what the work entailed, and I'd always thought Henry's job was interesting. Could I land a job as a county extension agent, working with rural people? That sounded like something I would like to do.

Thanks to my research assistantship money, I didn't need an outside job, so I immersed myself in my studies and my research. I had a study desk on the top floor of Agriculture Hall on the UW–Madison campus, along with other graduate students working on master's or PhD

Agriculture Hall on the University of Wisconsin campus
WHI IMAGE ID 55506

degrees. I became good friends with several of them. We all worked hard, but we also played. In the evenings, I learned to square dance in our study area in Ag Hall. During our noon breaks, a half dozen of us played poker using paper clips for chips.

One PhD student, Patrick Boyle, was friendly enough, but his actions suggested he saw our card playing and square dancing as so much foolishness. He preferred to stay working at his desk in the back corner of the attic. As it turned out, Pat Boyle would have considerable influence on my career in the coming years.

I enjoyed my year as a graduate student. But unlike several of my colleagues, I still had no aspirations to become a professor. When I finished my master's degree, I wanted to become a county agent, working with farm people.

But aspirations change, often in unexpected ways.

1 First Extension Job

In the spring of 1957, I learned that the position of 4-H agent was open in Green Lake County. By that time I had determined that being a county agent was the job for me, and I quickly decided to apply.

Most of what I knew about county agent work was from either a farmer's or a 4-H member's perspective, however, so I did some research. I learned that county extension workers were part of the University of Wisconsin's Cooperative Extension Service, which meant that in addition to being members of the College of Agriculture faculty, they were employed by the county in which they worked and by the United States Department of Agriculture. This three-way funding cooperation traced back to 1914, when the US Congress passed the Smith-Lever Act, creating the national Cooperative Extension Service with three budget sources: federal, state, and county. It was a complex funding structure requiring three units of government to cooperate, but it worked well.

On a cool April evening, I rode to Green Lake with Oscar Woelfel, director of extension's South Central District. I had already passed an initial screening by the

College of Agriculture extension committee in Madison and been invited to an interview with the Green Lake County Board's Agricultural Extension Committee. Typically the committee considered two candidates for these positions, and as Oscar drove along, he told me not to be disappointed if I didn't get the job. There were several other job openings I could apply for, he said. But I liked the possibility of working in Green Lake County. It was next to my home county, Waushara, and I had worked in the Green Lake County pea canneries during summers of my undergraduate college years. My dad bought farm equipment from the Sears and Roebuck store in Berlin, and my grandfather Apps had worked at a hotel in Green Lake when he first arrived from England.

The Green Lake County Extension Office was located in the county courthouse. After a brief wait, I was introduced to the Green Lake County Agricultural Extension Committee, which consisted of the chairman of the Green Lake County Board, Franklin Jahnke; the county superintendent of schools, Wilmer Gorski; a farm implement dealer from Berlin; and three other members of the county board.

In an interview lasting fifteen or twenty minutes, the committee seemed more interested in my farm background and the fact that I had been a 4-H member and leader than my five years of study at the university. They explained that the job largely entailed working with 4-H groups and told me I would also be assisting county ag agent G. Willys Gjermundson (called Willie) and home economics agent LaVerne Priebe on various projects.

I couldn't tell from their faces how I was doing during the interview. Afterward, I sat alone in a little room in the basement of the Green Lake County Courthouse,

THE WISCONSIN IDEA

It was while researching the University of Wisconsin's Cooperative Extension Service that I first became acquainted with the term "the Wisconsin Idea."

The Wisconsin Idea is a University of Wisconsin tradition that has its origins in the 1870s, when university president John Bascom informed students that they "had a moral duty to share their expertise broadly."[1] It has long been a guiding philosophy for the university, representing a commitment to using the work of the UW for the public good.

UW president Charles Van Hise said in a 1904 speech, "I shall never be content until the beneficent influence of the University reaches every home in the state."[2] Van Hise was instrumental in creating an extension division with courses and programs designed for the state's citizens. The UW established an agricultural extension service in 1908, with the first county agricultural extension agent assigned to Oneida County in 1912. Van Hise's friendship with Governor Robert M. La Follette led to close ties between the university and state government, and UW faculty worked with lawmakers to forge such progressive reforms as the nation's first workers' compensation laws and regulation of utilities.

It was in 1912 that the phrase "the Wisconsin Idea" first appeared in print. In his book with that title, state legislative librarian Charles McCarthy described problems facing the country and advocated for the use of University of Wisconsin resources to address them. In an introduction to the book, President Theodore Roosevelt wrote, "[I]n Wisconsin there has been a successful effort to redeem the promises by performances, and to reduce theories into practice. . . . The Wisconsin reformers have accomplished the extraordinary results for which the whole nation owes them so much, primarily because they have not confined themselves to dreaming dreams and then to talking about them."[3]

As the years passed, the meaning of "the Wisconsin Idea" became much broader, serving as a motto for the state's far-reaching commitment to public service. By the 1930s, the Wisconsin Idea was usually explained with the phrase, "The boundaries of the campus are the boundaries of the state."[4]

Growing up, I had never heard of the Wisconsin Idea. But I saw it in practice. Two UW–Madison county extension agents worked out of Wautoma, the county seat for Waushara County: an agricultural agent, who brought UW research and applications to farmers, and a home economics agent, who did the same for farm women. Both worked with farm kids through the 4-H program. I remember the county agricultural agent, Henry Haferbecker, stopping by the farm to talk with my father. Those conversations involved the management of our small dairy herd, new forage varieties, and the advantages of growing hybrid corn. When I was ten and therefore old enough to join 4-H, I experienced the Wisconsin Idea firsthand when I studied the 4-H bulletins written at the College of Agriculture in Madison and participated in the many activities organized by our county extension agents, including animal judging and speaking contests. I could not have known then that the Wisconsin Idea would become an important foundation for my career and my teaching philosophy.

NOTES
1. "The Wisconsin Idea," University of Wisconsin,
   https://wisconsinidea.wisc.edu/history-of-the-wisconsin-idea.
2. Ibid.
3. Charles McCarthy, *The Wisconsin Idea* (New York: The Macmillan Company, 1912),
   vii–viii
4. "The Wisconsin Idea," University of Wisconsin.

My first extension office was in the basement of the Green Lake County Courthouse.

wondering whether I had gotten the job. I was relieved it was over, as this was the first time I had been interviewed for a job in such a formal manner. (When I applied for a summer job as a pea viner boss in Markesan a few summers before, the interview questions had consisted of whether I knew how to fix stuff and whether I owned a crescent wrench.)

Finally, Oscar Woelfel came to retrieve me. He said nothing. This had to be a bad sign.

When I returned to the conference room, Franklin Jahnke held out his hand and said, "Congratulations, you are our new 4-H agent." I sat down at the table, and the committee began discussing my salary.

County board member Henry Losinski, a farmer with red hair and a tanned, wrinkled face, had not asked one question during the entire interview. Now he said, "I want you to know that just because you have a master's degree doesn't mean you get more pay."

I didn't reply.

It was clear that the committee had already discussed my salary and had a number in mind. I didn't know what to expect, but I did know that new high school agriculture instructors with twelve-month appointments were receiving $5,200 annually. And I knew the county was responsible for providing an office, secretarial assistance, office supplies, and a portion of each agent's salary—so ideally each of the governmental bodies involved (the USDA, the university, and the county) provided one-third of the cost of operating a county extension office. The USDA portion of the salary was managed by and combined with the university's contribution. The county managed its salary contribution separately. Thus, county extension employees received two checks, one from the university and one from the county in which they worked.

"We're prepared to offer you $4,600 a year, six days' paid vacation after you've worked a year, and an expense account to cover your travel costs. The office is open from eight to five Monday through Friday, and from eight to twelve on Saturday. And you'll also be working many evenings. Is all of this agreeable to you?" asked Franklin Jahnke.

I said it was—though I was thinking about that $5,200 new high school ag teachers were earning. Later I learned that the salaries of extension workers were based on the tax base of the county; larger, more prosperous counties paid higher salaries. Green Lake was relatively small, and its contribution to my salary was one hundred dollars per month. (Later that year, when the annual salaries for most county workers were printed in the newspaper, mine was listed as $1,200. I received several offers of potatoes and other food from folks unaware of the additional money I received from federal and university sources.)

The committee told me to report for work at 8 a.m. on Monday, June 17. Before Oscar and I headed back to Madison, Willie gave me a tour of the county extension offices crowded into a corner of the Green Lake County Courthouse's basement. He showed me his office and the office I would share with LaVerne Priebe, the home economics agent, who had been there only a few months. I saw the outer office and the secretary's desk—the three of us would share one secretary. And he told me that my first day of work was a cleanup day at Camp Patrick Lake in Adams County. I should come to the office wearing work clothes.

That spring I finished my graduate courses and compiled my research findings; I was one of the first in the department to use a computer for this task. I turned in my master's thesis with the inspiring title "Characteristics of Youth Choosing Farming as an Occupation in Five Selected Counties in Wisconsin." I received my master of science degree in June.

With the little money I had left from my year of graduate work, I bought a used blue 1953 Nash Ambassador, commonly described as an upside-down bathtub. It was a big car, it was cheap, and it got me from here to there. Willie Gjermundson had told me that if I needed housing I should get in touch with Mrs. Walker, who owned a big rooming house in Green Lake where the county's social worker, another single fellow, also lived. Mrs. Walker agreed to rent me an upstairs room in her big house. It was a larger room than I'd had in Madison, but nothing fancy. I would have to take my meals at the local restaurant.

On a clear, cool Monday morning, I parked my big blue Nash by the back door of the courthouse, walked down the steps, and entered the Green Lake County Extension Office. The outer office was nearly filled with people, all chatting with Jeannette, the secretary, and with Willie and LaVerne. I wondered if I was late and glanced at my watch: 7:40. Technically, I was twenty minutes early. But I quickly learned that if you arrived at the office at 8:00 a.m., you were late.

I was introduced all around and discovered that the people gathered there were volunteer 4-H leaders prepared to travel to the Patrick Lake 4-H camp in Adams County, about an hour's drive west of Green Lake. Camp Patrick Lake, located on a small lake with the same name, had been a Civilian Conservation Corps camp. It was closed during World War II and then reopened as a 4-H camp. The camp had two bunkhouses and a mess hall with a kitchen at one end. It had electricity but no indoor plumbing. The one source of fresh water was a hand-operated pump located between the mess hall and the bunkhouses.

When we arrived at the camp, Willie listed the cleanup chores: scrubbing down the mess hall, cleaning the kitchen, taking down and cleaning the stovepipes for the wood-burning cookstove, sweeping out the bunkhouses, and washing all the windows. "And digging new pits for the outdoor toilets," he said with a smile.

People began volunteering for the various tasks—but nobody volunteered for digging toilet pits. "I'll dig toilet pits," I said, grabbing one of the shovels we had brought along. Everyone stopped to look at me. I was sure I knew what they were thinking: what does this young new 4-H agent know about digging a toilet pit? What they didn't know was that I had grown up without indoor plumbing and had dug more than one toilet pit during my growing-up years on the farm. I gained the respect of my new colleagues and the volunteers that day, and it would serve me well, as I would work with many of them in the years to come.

Back in the office the next day, Willie showed me the files for the various county 4-H clubs. Then he pointed out the assorted UW College of Agriculture and USDA bulletins available free to local farmers. Topics ranged from growing corn to raising beef, from caring for strawberries to canning green beans. Bulletins for 4-H members, ages ten to twenty-one, were also available, on dairy, forestry, food preparation, clothing, woodworking, tractor maintenance, poultry, soil conservation, field crops, and more.

"I'm not one for giving out advice," Willie said, "but one thing I've learned is, the more time you spend out of this office, the better. We work with people, and we go where the people live. The office files can wait." It was good advice. I got in my car and spent much of my time for the next several weeks driving around the county, stopping to meet with volunteer 4-H leaders and to look at members' gardens, calves, cooking and canning, and sewing and other homemaking projects. I drank lots of coffee and ate cookies of every kind. I drove south to Markesan and Manchester and Dalton, visited with folks on the Mackford Prairie, headed north to meet those around Berlin and Princeton, and stopped in at Ripon. Checking the records, I noticed that there were few 4-H members in the Princeton area. When I asked around, someone said, "You'd better talk to the priest at St. John the Baptist."

The Princeton area had many farmers of Polish heritage, and they all attended St. John the Baptist Catholic Church. I made an appointment to visit with the priest, a tall, friendly fellow. We chatted a bit about my background and my new job as 4-H agent, and I quietly inquired about why there were no 4-H clubs in the Princeton area. His response surprised me. "Tell me," he asked, "how is 4-H different from Hitler's youth corps? Isn't 4-H also a government-inspired youth movement?"

Technically he was correct. 4-H clubs are a part of the Cooperative Extension Service, which means they are a part of federal, state, and county government. But I assured him 4-H was not a political program meant to indoctrinate young people, but rather was an educational program. I gave examples of projects the young members took on, and I mentioned such 4-H activities as the county fair, camps, music, and drama programs. As we talked I listened carefully, but I couldn't tell if I was answering his question in a way that satisfied his concerns.

A couple of weeks later, I got a call from a farmer near Princeton asking if I would come out to his farm to meet with several young people and their parents about the possibility of organizing a 4-H club. The farmer concluded our conversation with: "Father said he thought 4-H sounds like a good program for the parish's children." Later I learned that the priest had been a displaced person from Poland and had seen firsthand the workings of the Hitler youth corps. The community soon had an active 4-H club.

A few weeks into my new job, it was time for the Green Lake County Fair. Willy, LaVerne, and I, along with several volunteers, were responsible for everything that happened at the fair. My duties mainly involved the 4-H projects members exhibited there. At the county highway department garage and its parking lot, young people from throughout the county displayed their 4-H projects, including dairy and beef calves, sheep and hogs, chickens and ducks, clothing and food entries, and woodworking projects such as birdhouses and door-stops. All were judged and awarded a blue (first place), red (second), white (third), or pink (fourth) ribbon.

WCWC, a new radio station in nearby Ripon, was broadcasting from the fair, and I did several interviews with Jim Densmore, the newly hired farm radio broad-caster. Later WCWC would invite me to appear on a regu-lar radio show, which I did for the two and a half years I worked in Green Lake County.

Several local companies had rented exhibit space at the fair to show off their products. As I strolled through the exhibits, one selling travel trailers caught my eye. I had a long talk with the owner, a Mr. Happersett, and I learned I could buy a twenty-four-by-eight-foot Mallard travel trailer for $2,400. Unfortunately, that was more than half my annual salary. But I could dream. My little second-floor room in Mrs. Walker's rooming house was a decent enough place, but if I could scrape together a 10 percent down payment for the trailer, I could do my own cooking and save the money I was spending at the local restaurant.

For the next few months I saved as much as I could, and by September I was the proud owner of a twenty-four-foot Mallard travel trailer with one bedroom, a small bathroom, and a pleasant eating, studying, and reading area at the front end. It had a propane cookstove, an electrical hookup for lights, a refrigerator, and a fan for a tiny fuel oil furnace. I rented a spot at a trailer park just outside the village of Green Lake. The rent included the water and sewage hookup and the cost of the electricity. I decided against a telephone; I could always use the phone at my office, which was only a mile away.

Now, after a long day on the road filled with meetings of one kind or another, it was wonderful to return to the quiet of my little trailer, prepare something to eat, and read or listen to the radio. I could fix my own meals, including my noon lunch, which I carried to work with me. One of the great benefits of the courthouse office in Green Lake was its location on a lake, and I kept a fishing pole leaning in one corner of my office. On a slow day, after eating lunch I often fished for a half hour or so.

In August I was off to Camp Patrick Lake for a week of fun and education. I was camp director for twenty-five or thirty 4-H members, half girls and half boys, ages twelve to sixteen, who stayed overnight at camp. We also offered day camping for the younger children, ages ten and eleven, and special overnight camping for those seventeen and older. I called evening square dances (thanks to my third-floor Agriculture Hall training), told tall tales around a campfire (a skill I'd learned from my father), and led nature hikes. I was responsible for all that happened at the camp, with the exception of the food preparation, handled by the camp cook. LaVerne Priebe also attended camp, helping the cook prepare three meals a day on a wood-burning cookstove and instructing the children on craft projects.

I was anxious about the morning and afternoon swimming times, as we had no lifeguard. For each session I rowed a boat to the edge of the swimming area and watched carefully while the kids had fun in the water. Keeping an eye on thirty kids, when I could sometimes see only their heads, proved a challenge.

One morning I glanced toward the middle of the lake, and there I saw a kid's head bobbing up and down. He had violated my rule to stay within the swimming area. I yelled at him to swim back toward shallower water. I saw that he had a big smile on his face, increasing my frustration with the rule-breaker.

"I'm standing on the bottom," he yelled back to me.

I hadn't realized the lake was so shallow. I don't remember the punishment I gave the young man, but I do recall that everyone in camp had a good laugh.

The days and months flew by as I worked fifty- or sixty-hour weeks, usually including both Saturday and Sunday. LaVerne left the county in the spring of 1958, and her replacement, Betty Hoag, did not arrive until February of 1959. So for the better part of a year, Willie and I were not only doing our work but also trying to keep the home economics program alive. I also had to keep up with my army correspondence courses and attend a two-week army summer camp, but I managed to fit it all in—and indeed was enjoying it immensely. In addition to my radio appearances, I had begun writing a weekly column for the *Berlin Journal* about 4-H happenings. I also called square dances for 4-H gatherings, recruited and trained volunteer 4-H leaders, and assisted Willie with his agriculture programs.

In the winter of 1957–1958, I attended an evening meeting in Markesan. When I left to drive back to Green Lake, it was a clear night, but cold—fifteen below zero. I hadn't gone five miles out of Markesan when the big blue Nash began to wheeze. Then I saw an immense cloud of steam lift from under the hood. I knew the Nash was about to die, right there in the middle of nowhere on a country road that had no traffic. I pulled off to the side, got out, and lifted the hood. A geyser of hot steam collided with the cold night. I glanced at my watch and saw that it was 10:30 p.m. I knew any farmer in the area was likely in bed. I began walking. Thankfully, I had a warm coat and a cap with ear flaps, but within a quarter of a mile I was freezing. A half mile or so ahead, I could see a light. I trudged on, leaving behind the still-steaming Nash. After far too long, I walked up the driveway to a very dark farmhouse, hoping the cold night meant the farm dog was inside and not prepared to gallop down the driveway and bite me on the leg.

I knocked on the door. Sure enough, a dog began barking loudly. Then an upstairs light came on, and soon I was greeted by a very unhappy-looking farmer. I told him who I was and what had happened. By this time his wife had joined him. They ushered me into the house and sat me down by their oil-burner stove to warm up while we talked about my predicament. Soon the farmer was pulling on his winter coat and cap, a jug filled with water at the ready, and we were in his pickup driving back to my stalled car.

"Something probably happened to your thermostat," the farmer said as he opened the now cooled radiator and poured it full of water.

I started the Nash, thanked the farmer profusely, and made my way back to Green Lake without incident. I had to drain the water from the radiator when I got back to my trailer, as it would surely freeze on such a frigid night. It was well past midnight when I got to bed. The next day I traded the Nash for a new red Nash Rambler. Now I had two monthly payments, one for a car and one for my trailer. I'd found out why the blue Nash had been on the used-car market with low mileage. And I had renewed faith in the

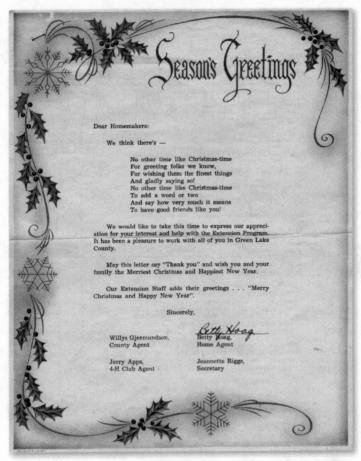

Each Christmas season, the Green Lake County extension staff mailed a holiday newsletter to homemakers throughout the county.

goodness of people, evidenced by that couple willing to help a stranded 4-H agent on a below-zero night.

The following October, at a monthly district extension meeting in Portage, I met Ruth Olson, a spring 1959 graduate of Stout State University (now UW–Stout) and a temporary home economics agent for Sauk County in

Baraboo, about sixty miles from Green Lake. At the fall conference later that month, an annual event where all the extension agents in the state gathered for a week of training and an evening of fun, I decided Ruth was someone I would like to get to know better. We had been dating for about a month when Waushara County, my home county, hired Ruth as a full-time home economics agent. Now our homes were within thirty miles of each other.

And then everything changed again. George Dehnert, the director of the extension's northeast district, called me. "Would you be interested in interviewing for the open 4-H and livestock agent position in Brown County?"

My colleagues and I all knew about the "plum" places to work for extension, and Brown County was on the list (along with Dane, Fond du Lac, Winnebago, Marathon, and a couple of others). The salaries at those locations were considerably higher, but so were the work expectations, as the farm population was substantial in those counties. The number of 4-H clubs would be about double that of Green Lake County, and along with running the 4-H program I would be responsible for educational programs for beef, sheep, and hog farmers.

I agreed to be interviewed. But when I found out who my competition was for the job—a more experienced agent from a western county—I decided I was the token agent filling the requirement that the committee have a minimum of two people from which to choose. Still, it would be nice to spend the day in bustling Green Bay, which had a population of about fifty thousand in those days (Green Lake's population was fewer than a thousand). And I would do my best at the interview, even though I knew the job was destined for someone else.

2 Brown County Extension

The Brown County Agricultural Extension Committee met in a conference room on the second floor of the newly constructed Federal Building, across the street from the Brown County Courthouse on East Walnut Street. The post office was on the first floor, and federal offices and the county extension office were on the second floor, along with offices for the Soil Conservation Service and the FBI.

The interview room was hot and stuffy, and I quickly developed a major headache. The interview took nearly an hour, with lots of probing questions about my background in animal science, my experience with radio, my work with TV (almost none at that time), my interest in writing columns, and more. It was an exhausting afternoon. As I waited for the committee's decision, I couldn't wait to hear that I'd been turned down so I could drive back to my comfortable little trailer, put my feet up, and enjoy a cold beer.

Then George Dehnert called me back in the room. He had a strange look on his face. He told me that the other candidate had already left for his home in western Wisconsin.

The committee chair shook my hand and congratulated me. He asked if I would accept a salary of $7,200, plus
my own private office, my own secretary, and an ample
expense account. By this time my Green Lake salary had
climbed to $5,800. I almost answered, "Are you sure?"

Instead I said yes—and immediately began to feel
overwhelmed. My predecessor, Ernie Ehrbar, had taken
a job as agricultural agent for Sheboygan County. He was
well respected in Brown County and had been doing
an excellent job. Was I prepared to fill his rather large
shoes? I wasn't at all sure. And what about Ruth? Green
Bay is about ninety miles from Wautoma. Would this be
the end of our relationship?

I drove back to Green Lake, my headache even worse
than before. I wondered if I had made the right decision.
Everything was going well in Green Lake; I knew the
county and knew the people. Ruth and I saw each other
nearly every weekend. What was I thinking? I wondered
if I should tell George Dehnert I didn't want the Brown
County job after all. But I knew that would likely be the
end of any promotion opportunities.

I could tell Ruth was not too happy about my decision to move to Green Bay. She congratulated me on my
new job, but with little enthusiasm. Later, after I reas-
sured her that I would visit Wautoma as many weekends
as I could, she seemed happier. My colleagues at the
Green Lake extension office weren't pleased with the
news either, for now they would have to break in a new
4-H agent.

In November, I took a day's vacation and drove
to Green Bay to meet the extension office staff: Dick
Schuster, county agricultural agent and office chair; June
Billings, county home economics agent; Doris Staidl,

consumer marketing agent; and Larry Tlachac, farm and home development agent. I also met my secretary, Judy Nelson, and had a chance to see the layout of the offices, including mine, which was larger than the one I shared with LaVerne Priebe in Green Lake.

I'd looked at the names of the staff members before arriving, but I did not know how to pronounce them all. Schuster was easy, so was Billings, and even Staidl. But Tlachac is where I made a major faux pas. When I stopped at Larry's office, I extended my hand and said, "So nice to meet you, Mr. *ta-lack-hack*." "It's *claw-hutch*," Larry said, not smiling. Unlike my home in central Wisconsin, the area around Brown and Door Counties has a considerable population of people of Belgian heritage—Larry Tlachac among them. We quickly moved on to talk about his work helping farm families with their records and business plans. Doris Staidl's job was also new to me: she appeared on radio and TV to teach food preparation, home management, and related skills. In addition, Doris wrote regular food columns for the *Green Bay Press Gazette* and for the county's weekly newspapers. About once a week she was on one or more of the county's radio stations, talking about nutrition and food preparation.

I met Elsa Stanek, head secretary and office administrator. She was friendly and outgoing, and she had the uncanny ability, I later learned, to know where every person on the staff was at any time and what programs they had coming up. It was a sizeable task, with five professional extension people working in all parts of the county and in and out of the office all the time.

While visiting with Dick Schuster, who would be my supervisor, I learned about media outlets in Green Bay: three UHF-TV stations, several radio stations, the daily

Green Bay Press Gazette, and several weekly newspapers. He said I was expected to write a weekly column for the daily paper and a different weekly column for the weekly papers; I would also do at least one radio program a week and two or three TV shows a month. He asked if I had any problems with doing so much media work. I told him no. In fact, I looked forward to this part of the job, as I liked writing, had gotten some experience with radio in Green Lake, and was eager to learn about TV work.

Dick also told me about the county livestock program. "We have but a few farmers raising sheep, but a good number raise beef cattle, and even more have hogs." Dick worked with dairy farmers, the county's major agricultural activity. He said the staff worked together on many projects, including 4-H camps, the county fair, and the Northeast Wisconsin Livestock Show. He also mentioned that the office was receiving many urban calls about trees, shrubs, and flower gardening that I would help with.

When I explained to Dick that I couldn't move my trailer until spring, he suggested I rent a long-term room at the nearby YMCA. As an aside, he told me that Vince Lombardi had been hired as the new coach of the Green Bay Packers, and the community was expecting great things from the team. It was evident that everyone I met was a Packers fan.

Back in Green Lake, I started making the transition from one job to the next—never an easy process. I looked forward to new challenges but was sad to leave behind good friends. By November, Green Lake County had hired my replacement, Roland Manthe, who would begin January 1, 1960. I tried to make sure my files were in decent order; I had taken Willie's advice and had not spent much time with filing, and Jeannette had enough to do without working on my files.

On January 3, a Sunday, I moved into the Green Bay YMCA. My second-floor room was considerably smaller than my trailer, and even smaller than the room I had rented at the Walker rooming house in Green Lake. The building was about half-full of longtime residents, some single young men, some older men down on their luck— an interesting mixture of male humanity. I introduced myself to one of my new neighbors, a middle-aged fellow in need of a shave. "Say, if you are looking for a whorehouse, I know about one in Upper Michigan," he offered. "Prices are right." I smiled and said I wasn't interested.

I reported for work at 7:45 on a cold Monday morning. Dick Schuster was already at work, and I soon learned from him that everyone on the staff was expected to be at our desks by 8:00 every morning, no matter how late we got home from an evening meeting—and there were many of those. "I want to make sure that if anyone from the County Board Agriculture Extension Committee stops by at eight, they'll see us at our desks and at work," Dick explained. "Some taxpayers don't have a very good opinion of county workers."

My first week on the job, I met Orion Samuelson, farm broadcaster for Green Bay's WBAY-TV, when he interviewed me on air about my background and my early impressions of Green Bay. I learned how to do live TV shows from Orion, as there was no videotaping in 1960. He had (and still has) a wonderfully deep radio-TV voice, knew the agriculture of the area, and was respected and well-liked by everyone who watched his noon TV show, which was nearly all the farmers in the county and well beyond. I didn't know it at the time, but we were the same age: both twenty-six that year.

Soon I was doing weekly TV shows with Orion. One time I asked him how we knew if anyone was watching the show. He chuckled and said, "Lots of people are watching. But one way to check is to offer people something for free and have them write in for it."

On my next show I talked about how bluebird numbers were dwindling and the importance of building bluebird nesting boxes. I announced that anyone who wanted free plans for how to build a nesting box should send a postcard to the TV station with the request. Within a week, we received 125 postcards, and my secretary was busy sending out bluebird house construction directions.

Nearly every Friday, the radio and TV farm broadcasters, the farm news writers, the extension office agriculture workers (Schuster, Tlachac, and me), and the Soil Conservation Service person met for coffee to discuss what was going on in Brown County agriculture. As a result, I had an excellent relationship with all the extension media people. At one of our regular meetings that summer, Orion said he had an announcement to make. "I've been offered a farm broadcasting position at WGN in Chicago," he said. We were all taken aback. His viewers in northeastern Wisconsin loved him, and we couldn't imagine him leaving Brown County and WBAY.

Being the newcomer to the group, and probably because I didn't know any better, I asked, "What kind of salary did they offer you?"

"Ten thousand dollars a year," Orion said. We all agreed that it would take that kind of money for any of us to move to Chicago. We wished him well, and we missed him greatly after he left. (At this writing Orion continues to work for WGN in Chicago and has a national and international reputation for his agricultural broadcasting work. And he remains a friend.)

That same first week on the job in Green Bay, I met Ray Pagel, the farm editor for the *Green Bay Press Gazette*, for whom I would be writing a weekly column. Ray was an old-school journalist, gruff and outspoken, and an excellent writer and editor. Having written columns for more than two years for the *Berlin Journal*, I thought I knew something about column writing. But after submitting my first column to Ray, I thought I was back in my college English classes. He had circled words and phrases, crossed out others, moved things around, and in the margins wrote such notes as "Redundant," "What does this mean?" and "Straying from your theme." All with a red pen. Over time, though, I came to greatly appreciate Ray's help in improving my writing skills, and my weekly columns were well received.

When the weather warmed in the spring of 1960 and the snow had melted, I hauled my little house trailer to Green Bay and parked it in a trailer park on the east side. I had a home of my own again and was able to do my own cooking. I still did not have a phone or a television. A radio was good enough, and I had lots of books. Besides, when I got home at night from a meeting—nearly every evening there was one someplace in the county—I mostly wanted to sleep. I knew I must be at my desk at eight the following morning, wide awake or not.

That summer I served as 4-H camp director for two weeklong camps, one for younger members and one for those sixteen and older. Camp Susan, near Antigo, was a vast improvement over the rather primitive Camp

Patrick Lake where Green Lake 4-H members camped. Camp Susan had indoor plumbing, a beautiful dining hall with a stone fireplace at one end, and a modern kitchen. The camp buildings overlooked a pristine lake. I had enough of a budget to hire a lifeguard, who was also the camp's recreational director.

The two dorms, one for girls and one for boys, had volunteer adult 4-H leader chaperones who slept there and made sure that everyone was in bed with lights out by the eleven o'clock curfew. One night at eleven, the girls' dorm chaperone came to me with the news that one of the girls was missing (I'll call her Jean). Soon the chaperone of the boys' dorm came to me with similar news: one of the boys was missing (let's call him Tom). Of course, we adults suspected what was going on, as we had seen Tom and Jean holding hands at the camp-fire earlier in the evening. I sent out a search party, and soon the two young lovers were found walking along the beach, oblivious to the fact that they had missed curfew.

It was up to me to decide their punishment. I asked the two of them to meet me in the little storage room that served as my temporary office. I knew I had to make an example of the pair, or we'd have more violations during the week. The last thing I wanted was for the parents of these young people to think our camp lacked discipline, especially when it came to late forays for young couples. But I was also sympathetic to the young people, knowing I would probably have done the same thing if I'd had the opportunity when I was their age. I had an idea.

Jean was crying when she came into the room; Tom looked like he was about to. Trying my best to be serious and stern, I said, "You know you have broken a camp rule?" They both nodded.

Speaking with a group of older 4-H members at Camp Susan

"We were just walking along the lake," Tom said.

"That's all we were doing," sobbed Jean.

"I really should tell your parents about this," I said, maintaining my serious demeanor. "What do you think your punishment should be?" I hadn't yet figured out what kind of punishment would be appropriate. They did not respond. "Tell you what," I said. "You both go to bed, and tomorrow morning after breakfast, you tell me what you think would be appropriate punishment for what you did."

They left, Jean still sobbing, Tom walking with his head down. The next morning after breakfast, the three of us met again. Neither of the two young people looked like they'd gotten much sleep. "Well, what have you decided?" I asked.

Tom spoke first. "We've agreed that I'll clean the boy's toilet every day."

"And I'll clean the girl's toilet every day," said Jean. "And both of us will scrub clean the stones around the fireplace in the dining hall."

I thought, *wow, that's far worse punishment than I could have come up with*, but I said, "Okay, if you do all of this, then I won't tell your parents." They did, and I didn't. And there were no curfew violations the remainder of the camp.

Ruth and I became engaged in November 1960 and were married on May 20, 1961. The week before our wedding, I conducted a dairy judging contest at the Green Bay Reformatory, which had a fine dairy herd. My favorite joke at the wedding and for years to come was that I was in prison the week before we married.

Ruth and I sold my trailer and used the money to pay for the furniture for a little house we rented on Cass Street in Green Bay. My workload continued to be heavy, but we found time to become more acquainted with Green Bay's history and wonderful foods that were new to us, such as chicken booyah (shredded chicken and vegetables in a broth), knee caps (sweet fried doughnuts without a hole but with an indentation in the middle filled with whipped cream), and kolaches (small Polish pastries with fruit preserves in the center). We also enjoyed the great polka dances on Saturday nights in dance halls in and around Green Bay.

Now I was doing two radio shows and a couple of live TV shows a week, writing two weekly newspaper columns, attending meetings, training 4-H leaders, and holding free educational meetings for hog and beef cattle farmers. It was easy to determine what content and teaching approaches resonated with the farmers invited to the programs. Let's say the topic was beef

One of my favorite tasks as a county 4-H agent was accompanying 4-H members to State 4-H Club Week in Madison.

cattle management strategies, and I had planned two one-hour sessions a week apart. I didn't need to have attendees fill out a fancy evaluation form to tell me how good (or bad) the program was. If thirty people came to the first session and only five people came to the second, I had my answer. Talking with farmer friends who attended the first session told me more. An important lesson learned: Farmers evaluate extension programs with their feet.

Phone calls to the office increased throughout the spring, summer, and fall of 1960, many of them about horticultural questions. When urban residents learned that extension agents would make house calls for everything from a dying shade tree to how to increase the yield of a strawberry bed, they called. Dick Schuster had more training in horticulture than I did, and he handled most

Helping young people become better acquainted with nature (here I'm holding a small snake) has always been one of my favorite teaching activities.

of the calls. But I took some of them, and one I remember vividly. An older woman called and said her plum tree just didn't look right; it was only July, and it was already beginning to drop some of its leaves. I riffled through several USDA bulletins on fruit trees to bone up a bit on plum tree challenges but found little information.

The woman was waiting for my arrival. "Do you know about plum tree difficulties?" she asked. "Yes," I replied, but not with enough confidence to impress her. I could tell by the look on her face that the situation was very serious for her. We rounded the corner of the house, and she pointed to a sickly little plum tree missing about half of its leaves. It was a sorry-looking specimen.

"What spray would you recommend I use to cure my little tree?" she asked.

"I wouldn't recommend spraying," I said.
"Oh? What would you recommend?"
"Pruning."
"Pruning?" She had a puzzled look on her face.
"Yes, pruning."
"Where and how much?"

I often met individually with volunteer 4-H leaders. Here I am
meeting with leader Bill Hock to discuss Brown County's tractor
maintenance 4-H project.

"I'd recommend pruning this plum tree level with the ground," I said with as much authority as I could muster.

"You mean—destroy it?"

"Yes. It's beyond saving."

"Well, I will do no such thing," she said. Her face was red, and had her garden rake been handy, I think she would have swung it at me. I hurried to my car and drove back to the office.

When I arrived, Dick called me into his office. "You just get back from a plum tree call?" he asked. I said I had and that I had told the woman to cut down her tree because it couldn't be saved.

"That was probably the right answer, but you'll want to work a little on your garden-side manner," Dick said, laughing loudly. He had just gotten off the phone with the woman, who had described me as the most incompetent person she'd ever met.

It had not been one of my best days.

Another less-than-stellar day occurred in the fall, during the Northeast Livestock Show held at the Brown County fairgrounds in De Pere. Future Farmers of America and 4-H members from throughout northeast Wisconsin brought their sheep, beef cattle, and hogs to the show for judging. It was a large event, attracting hundreds of people, and because it was in Brown County I had a major role in organizing, promoting, and operating it, with help from some other extension agents in the region.

Chuck Ramsay, farm director at WLUK-TV, asked me if on the first day of the livestock show I would bring a competitor and his or her show animal to the noon news program. In those days, television studios were extremely warm under the bright lights, and I wondered

what kind of animal would do best in the strange setting. I ruled out hogs; they're too difficult to handle in
any situation. Steers: too big and too strong. I decided
on a lamb. They're small and easy to transport, and if one
of us held the lamb under its chin and by the stump of
its tail—the standard way of controlling a show lamb—we
should have no difficulty.

I selected a young 4-H member and her well-trained
Shropshire lamb. When we arrived at the station, I learned
that Alice in Dairyland, the Wisconsin dairy spokes-
person, would be joining us partway through the show.

We got rolling. The program was going well: the
bright lights and the warmth of the studio seemed
to make the lamb sleepy, so there was no danger of
it bolting off. The 4-H member had relaxed and was
readily answering questions. A few minutes into the
program, Alice in Dairyland was escorted onto the set,

In Brown County I helped teach 4-H members how to judge
dairy calves.

dressed in her usual gown and other finery. The young woman was apparently not very knowledgeable about lambs and their habits. She bent over to pet the little lamb, which was now very much awake. Alice had no more than gotten the words *Isn't this a cute little lamb* out of her mouth when the lamb took a huge bite out of her corsage. She let out a muffled shriek, and her face turned bright red. There was a moment of embarrassing silence as the lamb chewed on the mouthful of carnations and greens. To break the silence, I blurted out, "That lamb surely has good taste."

Alice in Dairyland's face burned even brighter. Chuck Ramsay's face turned white. The floor crew burst out into laughter, and the 4-H member began to snicker. After an agonizingly long time, the station flipped to a commercial. I, of course, never heard the last of it. The producer at WLUK jokingly later told me that the performance with the lamb had become the standard against which all other farm shows were measured. From that experience I learned to spend a moment thinking before I speak—a most important lesson that I try to follow to this day.

Shortly after arriving in Green Bay, I became active in the Green Bay Audubon Society. The organization partnered with our office in establishing bluebird trails for Brown County (a trail consisted of a half dozen or so bluebird houses strung in a line along a fencerow). I also worked with the Audubon Society to help farmers identify hilltops and odd corners that could not be cultivated but that would make great sanctuaries for birds and other wild animals. 4-H members helped establish several of these, some a few acres, some as small as a half-acre. The Audubon Society and the extension office had developed a mutual respect. But that relationship was challenged in 1962.

By the early 1960s, Dutch elm disease was on the rampage in Wisconsin. Researchers discovered that the disease was spread by the elm bark beetle. An effective way to stop the disease's spread was to spray elm trees with DDT (dichlorodiphenyltrichloroethane), a popular insecticide that many farmers used to control flies and municipalities used to control mosquitoes. In spring 1962, the Green Bay Street Department called on the extension office for advice on spraying elms, many of which lined the city's streets at the time. Dick Schuster passed along the information he had received from the UW College of Agriculture on when to spray and how much DDT to use on elm trees.

That same year, Rachel Carson's book *Silent Spring* had detailed DDT's devastating effects on the environment, especially birds. Many of us whose work involved the environment read the book, including DDT researchers at the College of Agriculture who chose to deny or question much of Carson's work. I knew one researcher who personally believed that DDT was safe and that it could and should be used for killing the elm bark beetle. In addition, UW administrators had gotten pushback from the tourism industry urging them to suppress Carson's findings. DDT spraying went on as planned. I felt like I was walking on a tightrope. I didn't agree with the College of Ag's DDT recommendations, and I refused to pass on their model news releases disparaging Rachel Carson's work. The college's recommendations had become sufficiently controversial that no one from the UW reprimanded me for my opposition to the use of DDT. Still, I'll never forget the day a friend with the Audubon

Society stopped by. She opened the little box she held to reveal several dead robins. "DDT did this," she said. All I could say was, "I know."

On June 28, 1962, our daughter, Susan, was born. That same week I had a call from Frank Campbell, the state 4-H leader, who worked out of offices in Agriculture Hall on the University of Wisconsin campus. "Would you be interested in the position of publications editor for the state 4-H office?" he asked. I knew about the many bulletins that UW–Extension wrote, edited, printed, and distributed to 4-H members and county extension offices throughout the state; we handed out many of them in Brown County. I knew that various College of Agriculture and School of Home Economics professors wrote the bulletins, on topics ranging from dairy cattle management to dress making, from foods and nutrition to woodworking. I also knew that the person currently in the publications editor position had a PhD in agricultural journalism. My degrees were in general agriculture and agriculture education. And although I had considerable experience writing, I had no editing experience whatsoever.

"I don't believe I'm qualified," I said. "I don't have a journalism degree."

"We know that," Campbell said. "But Director Ahlgren and I think you'll do well in this job, and we have staff in agricultural journalism who can teach you how to edit."

It seemed I was being offered the job without having to apply or interview. I told him I would have to talk it over with Ruth. Even though we had a newborn baby, the new job was appealing because it meant fewer night meetings and more time to spend with my family. Ruth asked, "Who are the other candidates for the position?" "No other candidates," I answered. We agreed to make the move. I had no idea how challenging the job would be.

3 Publications Editor

Ruth, baby Sue, and I arrived in Madison in late August 1962. We rented a little house on Park Lane on Madison's west side for $125 a month. Movers brought our furniture from Green Bay, and we settled into our new home.

On September 1, I reported to the University of Wisconsin campus for my new job. There was no written job description. Frank Campbell, my new boss, told me I would be responsible for editing and producing twelve to fifteen new bulletins each year and delivering them to county extension offices around the state. He also said that I would be doing some TV and radio work, but likely not as much as I had been doing in Green Bay, and I would give talks around the state to various 4-H groups, especially at 4-H leader recognition banquets. I quickly realized the job was much more than merely editing publications.

"What have I gotten myself into?" I wondered. My fellow extension agents around the state and I had often criticized the state 4-H office, especially the publications editor, for being slow in producing new bulletins. Now I would be the brunt of the criticism.

There were some positive notes about my new role, however. My new office—the largest one I'd had so far—was on the second floor of Agriculture Hall on the UW–Madison campus, with a great view of Lake Mendota. My salary had been bumped up to nine thousand dollars a year, and I was promoted from instructor to assistant professor in the College of Agriculture.

But I felt I was starting in a hole. Expectations for my new role were high. Would I be able to speed up the editing and production processes, especially when I knew almost nothing about editing, designing, and producing bulletins? Frank told me he had asked Professor Lloyd Bostian from the Agricultural Journalism Department if I could sit in on his bulletin editing class; I think Frank believed that after a few class sessions I would have the knowledge and skills I needed. How wrong he was.

My office staff, consisting of a copyeditor, a secretary, and a production person, had experience and were more than willing to show me what they were doing and how they did it. How fortunate I was to have such a skilled staff; they saved the day for me many times during my first few months on the job. By January of 1963 I was able to do a reasonable job of editing—my past writing experience and help from Ray Pagel at the *Green Bay Press Gazette* proved invaluable. But I quickly discovered that with just a master's degree, and one not in journalism, I carried little clout with the PhD professors who wrote the bulletins, especially those who believed that they were God's gift to the literary world and felt no one should dare to touch their perfect prose with an editing pen. After having my ears pinned back a time or two by these self-defined highly skilled authors, I learned that

COOPERATIVE EXTENSION SERVICE
in
AGRICULTURE AND HOME ECONOMICS

University of Wisconsin and United States Department of Agriculture Cooperating

H. L. AHLGREN
Associate Director
June 19, 1962

AGRICULTURAL HALL
Madison 6

Mr. Jerold W. Apps
Brown County 4-H Club Agent
Room 240 Federal Building
Green Bay, Wisconsin

Dear Mr. Apps:

This letter is being written to confirm our verbal understanding regarding the position which is open in the 4-H section on our state staff. The position is that of Assistant State 4-H Leader. The person in that position would have responsibility for our 4-H publications program.

It is my pleasure to invite you to consider accepting this position. We are in a position to offer you a starting salary of $9,000 on an annual basis effective August 15, 1962. You would hold the rank of Assistant Professor.

An early reply will be appreciated.

Sincerely yours,

Henry L. Ahlgren
Associate Director

When I became publications editor for the state 4-H Office in August 1962, I was also promoted to assistant professor.

my communication skills were as important as the editing work. I spent considerable time telling them about the 4-H members I had worked with in the past five years, describing what types of bulletins they liked and which did not serve them well. This approach helped, but it took time.

Another major challenge was getting the professors

to meet their deadlines. They had many other responsibilities, and I suspect that some of them—knowing their material would be heavily edited for use by young people—were even more reluctant to write for our office.

My goal was to produce well-edited and creatively designed bulletins. I had control over the editing and design, but the printing was done on the offset presses under the control of the Agricultural Journalism Department, and often I had to wait for the printing of a 4-H bulletin because a bulletin for adult farmers or home-makers was deemed of higher importance. Now I was not only spending lots of time with authors during the editing process, I was also spending time with those who decided the printing schedule, negotiating to make sure the 4-H bulletins were printed in a timely manner.

The printed bulletins were stored in an unheated former farm building located just beyond the old dairy barn on the ag campus. I employed two students, Peggy Ahlgren (daughter of Cooperative Extension Service director Henry Ahlgren) and a young man whose name I have forgotten, to sort, catalog, and track the bulletin inventory. The steel building was exceedingly hot in the summer, as it had no windows and no air conditioning, and in winter it was as cold inside as it was outside. But the students got the job done, with little complaining.

To distribute the bulletins to each of the seventy-two county offices, I arranged with the Ag College's farms office for one of their employees to deliver them in a university farms truck. Even the distribution system was not immune to criticism. One afternoon my secretary informed me that I had a phone call from Tom O'Connell, 4-H agent in La Crosse County—and that he was really angry.

CIRCULAR 4-H 122   AUGUST 1963

BETTER BREAKFASTS

UNIVERSITY of WISCONSIN Extension Service
College of Agriculture, Madison

The bulletins our publications team edited and produced covered a
range of topics, from "Better Breakfasts" to "Woodworking."

I knew Tom well from my time as a county agent.
"How are you, Tom?" I said when I picked up the phone.

"My 4-H bulletins just arrived," he said.

"That's good," I said.

"Do you know what happened?" he asked, his voice
rising.

I was almost afraid to ask, but I did. "What?"

"Your guy backed up to the La Crosse courthouse loading dock with the truck door open. He hit the loading dock a little too hard, and our 4-H bulletins spilled out in a big, tangled mess! What do you suggest I do?"

I knew I should be sympathetic, but I pictured a giant pile of spilled bulletins on the loading platform, and all I could think to say was, "I suggest you pick them up."

He hung up on me.

In the fall of 1963, Mitch Mackey, the personnel director for Wisconsin's Cooperative Extension Service, contacted me. "As you know, Director Ahlgren is working hard to have extension staff treated like other university faculty, both with comparable salaries and academic promotions," he told me.

"So I've heard." I was far too busy to give much thought to this new policy, but I had heard colleagues talk about it. We all welcomed the possibility that we might receive more pay.

"You've been in extension for six years," he said.

"Yes, that's right. I started in 1957."

"You need to apply for tenure, like other university assistant professors."

"You sure?" I answered. I didn't know much about tenure, what it meant, or why it was important.

"Yes, I'm sure. I'll fill out the forms for you, but you need to give me copies of what you've been writing and copies of the bulletins you've edited."

While working in Brown and Green Lake Counties, I had published a few articles in national 4-H publications and had written a pile of newsletters and newspaper columns. I gave copies of everything to Mitch and forgot about it. I was far too busy to worry about this elusive thing called tenure. A couple of months later, Mitch stopped by the office again. "You've got tenure," he told me, smiling.

I thanked him. But I didn't know then how important tenure was in a university setting. Later I would learn that achieving tenure usually meant promotion to associate professor and an increase in salary, though I received neither at that time because I did not have a PhD degree. I went back to editing and designing bulletins, something I was finally beginning to feel confident in my ability to do.

A year later, Walter Bjoraker, chair of the Department of Agricultural and Extension Education and my former undergraduate advisor, stopped by my office. We talked for a bit about my publications editor job. He told me the department was hiring new staff members since extension director Ahlgren had been working toward increasing the educational credentials of county extension people as one step toward them being accepted as bona fide faculty members of the University of Wisconsin's College of Agriculture. According to the new policy, the Department of Agricultural and Extension Education had become a lead department in helping county-based faculty interested in returning to the UW to complete a master of science degree. The number of graduate students in the department had increased rapidly.

Next he said, "As you've probably heard, the College of Agriculture has been working with Brazil to establish an agricultural college there."

"Yes, I've heard about that," I responded. The College of Agriculture was coordinating with both Nigeria and Brazil to establish agriculture teaching and research colleges in those countries. Selected faculty members spent two to three years working abroad with the new institutions, helping them become established.

"Well, Jim Duncan has accepted a two-year appointment there. And I was wondering if you would be interested in teaching Jim's Introduction to Extension course this fall." Walt told me that he had already talked to Frank Campbell about the administrative arrangement—the Department of Ag and Extension Education would transfer funds to the 4-H office to cover my teaching assignment. I would not receive any additional salary but would be taking on the class as a service to my old department.

I had taken the same course I was being asked to teach back in 1956, with Professor Duncan, and I remembered some of the content. I also had seven years' experience in extension that I could share with students.

"Jim left me a copy of his class notes, which you are free to use," Walt said. "You should be all set."

4 First Year of Teaching

At the beginning of the fall semester in 1964 I walked into a classroom on the first floor of Babcock Hall. Ten undergraduate students had enrolled in Agriculture and Extension 641: Introduction to Extension for three credits. This would be the first time I would teach a semester-long credit class (sixteen weeks, three times a week) in which I would be expected to not only provide content but also develop tests and give grades. As a county extension agent I had taught noncredit workshops, sometimes for a half day, sometimes three two-hour sessions spread over three weeks. The workshops were noncredit and involved no examinations or grading. And they were all highly practical: managing a beef herd, what's new in hog rations, how to get top dollar for your lambs at market. Now not only was I responsible for providing practical information for newly employed extension agents (most of my students had extension work as their career goal), but I would have time to develop and explore with students some of the theoretical and historical foundations for the ideas I was offering in class.

While I was a student at the University of Wisconsin, I had taken several courses devoted to how to teach and how to understand students. But as I thought about my own teaching approach, I realized that much of what I had learned on the farm had stayed with me, and I considered how effective my earliest teachers, and their methods, had been. My father, with only a fifth-grade education, and my mother, with a seventh-grade educa-

---

Agricultural and Extension Education 641
Cooperative Extension Work In Agriculture And Home Economics
University of Wisconsin, College of Agriculture

Fall Semester, 1964
Jerold W. Apps
205 Agricultural Hall

Objectives of the Course

General:

Have students develop an understanding, an appreciation and a working knowledge of the growth, nature, scope, operation and program results of Cooperative Extension Work.

Specific:

To have students:

1. Acquire knowledge and develop an understanding of the background conditions leading to the development and growth of the Extension Service.

2. Understand the organizational structure and the operation of the federal, state and county phases of the Cooperative Extension Service.

3. Understand the responsibilities of Extension personnel at state, district and county level.

4. Increase knowledge and understanding of the factors that contribute to learning.

5. Acquire knowledge about clientele groups.

6. Understand how Extension programs are planned.

7. Become acquainted with Extension methods and program evaluation.

8. Become aware of privileges and opportunities in Extension as a career.

Procedure

The class will meet three times a week for the semester. It will be conducted by lecture, class discussion, group work, individual assignments and field observations including a field trip to a nearby county.

The syllabus for the first credit course I taught, in the College of Agriculture during fall semester 1964

tion, were excellent teachers, although they surely never thought of themselves in that way. From my dad I learned how to split a block of wood, how to stand up grain bundles so they don't tip over in a rainstorm, and how to teach a calf to lead. When it comes to splitting wood, he said, before you lift the splitting maul you must spend a little time studying the block. Learn how to read it: study the direction of the wood grain and look for any knots that might cause problems. Decide where to start, where the block will split easiest. The more I thought about that lesson, the more it seemed to fit potential learners as well: I must get to know them, find the "direction of their grain" and where they may have "knots" that could get in the way of their learning.

I also learned a good deal about both critical and creative thinking from my father. When faced with a problem on the farm (they seemed to come up every day), my dad would tell me, "Figure it out." By that he meant examine it, think about it, and then come up with an answer or a solution—which might be a tried-and-true solution or one that no one else had thought about.

From my mother I learned the importance of telling the truth. I learned why your name is important, and how if you do something wrong the family's name would be tarnished forever, as people in rural communities have long memories. And I learned that it is important to be on time and to do things well no matter how much you dislike doing them.

I also thought about the teacher at our country school, Theresa Piechowski, and the strategy she used when teaching us how to read. I started school at age five, in 1939. There were about twenty of us representing all eight grades, with just two of us in first grade.

Eleanor and Herman Apps, my first teachers

When it was time for reading instruction, here's what Miss Piechowski did for me and the other first-grader, Norman Hudziak. She spread a long, narrow piece of paper, six feet or so long, on the floor in front of the bookshelves that made up the school's library. She drew lines across the paper, and on each line she wrote a word. She then gave each of us a little toy car and said, "This is a road, and to travel down the road, you must name each word that you come to." What fun it was to learn how to read this way. By Christmastime I was able to read words in our first-grade books, where I learned all about Dick, Jane, and Baby Sally in the Dick and Jane series. With Miss Piechowski's example, I discovered that learning was more fun than just about anything a little farm kid could do. I'd also never had a little toy car before, and the idea of driving one down a road of words was so fun and interesting, I hardly knew I was learning.

I thought about these early learning experiences as I studied the notes that Walt Bjoraker had given me—several hundred pages of them in a manila folder. They were handwritten on yellow sheets of lined paper, in Jim Duncan's scrawl that I'm sure even he had difficulty deciphering, and they were largely a mystery to me. Not only was I apprehensive about teaching a college-level semester-long course, but now I was faced with figuring out what to teach. Thankfully, I still had the notes I had taken when I took the course in the fall of 1956. But this was eight years later, and a good deal happens in an organization in that length of time. I soon discovered that I was spending hours preparing for the course—in addition to time spent in the classroom, grading papers, and preparing for and correcting examinations.

The class was not open to freshmen, so my students were mostly sophomores with a sprinkling of juniors and one or two seniors. Despite all the extra work associated with the course, on top of the challenges of editing, designing, producing, and distributing 4-H bulletins, giving speeches around the state, and doing some TV and radio work, I enjoyed the teaching experience. No one was telling me exactly what or how to teach. And most important, by working with the same students over an extended period of time on one topic, I was able to develop ideas in depth. Because of my interest in history, I created a unit on the history of informal off-campus university education, of which Cooperative Extension was an important component. I developed another on teaching strategies for informal education, using my experience in conducting educational programs via TV, radio, newspaper columns, face-to-face workshops, one-on-one contacts, and farm and home visits. The weeks flew by; I don't recall when I had ever been busier, felt more challenged, or had more fun.

Pat Boyle, with whom I had shared the graduate student room in the attic of Agriculture Hall back in 1956–57, was now a professor in the Department of Agricultural and Extension Education. I saw him frequently, and every time I did, Pat would say, "When are you going to start working on a PhD?"

My usual response was, "I haven't thought about it."

"Well, you should start thinking about it," Pat would say. He was well aware that to advance in higher education I needed a PhD.

In November of 1964, near the end of the fall semester, Walt Bjoraker stopped by my office again. I had seen him from time to time in the halls, and he had inquired about how the course was going. But now he came into my office and closed the door behind him. I had a sinking feeling that I had done something seriously wrong with my class. But what I heard was just the opposite. "I've been hearing good things from the students in your class," Walt said.

"I'm glad to hear it," I responded. I was waiting for the "but" that usually comes at this point in a conversation.

"We've had a discussion in the department, and we're wondering if you would consider becoming a full-time member of the Department of Agricultural and Extension Education."

The question came as a total surprise to me, as I had been assuming that when the fall semester ended, so would my college teaching career, and I would return to my duties as a full-time publications editor for the state 4-H office.

Walt continued, "I heard last week from Jim Duncan that he plans to stay another year in Brazil. So I talked to Dean Pound, and he gave me permission to hire an additional assistant professor in the department. Are you interested?"

I was so unprepared for the question that for several seconds I said nothing. Finally, I said I was interested but I would have to talk with Ruth. Since accepting the position would mean I'd be leaving the state 4-H office, I also wanted to talk with Frank Campbell and extension director Henry Ahlgren before I gave Walt an answer.

As I drove home from work that afternoon, my mind was filled with conflicting thoughts. I'd worked hard to learn how to edit and produce bulletins, and I had developed a good working relationship with most of the faculty who wrote them and staff members in charge of printing and production. My small office staff had developed a functional schedule for publishing bulletins, and the complaints from the counties had mostly disappeared. I also reflected on how much I was enjoying teaching a college-level course. Once again I was being offered a job that I had not applied for—never even interviewed

for—and that had no written job description. I also did
not have the basic credential, a PhD, that I thought all
new hires on the Madison campus were required to have.

That night I talked with Ruth about the possibility of
yet another job move—one that this time did not require
the family to move and meant I would move no farther
than across the hall in Ag Hall, though I would lose my
wonderful view of Lake Mendota. I didn't know the salary, but I expected it would be an increase. By this time
we had three children: Sue was two, Steve was one, and
Jeff was just a baby. Ruth was extremely busy at home
taking care of them, and we both knew that a pay increase
for me would help our family. We had recently purchased
a home on Madison's west side, and we were always short
of money. Ruth said the job move was fine if it was what
I wanted to do.

When I met with Frank Campbell, he said I would
be missed but that he understood my wanting a new
challenge. Besides, he noted, I would still be close at
hand to work with the person who replaced me. Henry
Ahlgren was less sure the job move was a good one for
me. He tried to convince me to reconsider and said other
job opportunities would be available for me if I kept a
100 percent Cooperative Extension appointment. But he
said he wouldn't stand in the way if this was something I
wanted to do.

I met with Glenn Pound, dean of the College of Agriculture. Dean Pound knew I didn't have a PhD degree,
and he was reluctant to approve the appointment.
Nevertheless, after looking over the papers Walt Bjoraker
had prepared, the dean looked up and said to me, "I'll
approve this, but you will not be promoted to associate
professor, nor will you receive an increase in salary,

until you complete a doctorate. We'll set your salary at ten thousand dollars. Do you agree?"

The salary was a thousand dollars more than I was earning at the state 4-H office. I gulped, thought for a moment, and said yes. I immediately wondered what Ruth's reaction would be when I told her I'd have to return to graduate school. It was against university policy for me to earn a degree in the same college where I taught, so I would either have to take a leave of absence or study at a different UW college or a different university entirely. What would we do for money during that time? We were barely making ends meet.

With those financial concerns very much on my mind, I began my position in the Department of Agricultural and Extension Education on January 1, 1965. My appointment was 25 percent resident instruction (teaching two courses a year, plus a four-week summer course, all on campus) and 75 percent extension work, helping with staff training and development. With extension staff scattered throughout the state, the staff development part of my job required a considerable amount of travel.

The Department of Curriculum and Instruction in the School of Education on the Madison campus accepted me for graduate work in the fall of 1964. The C and I department had a small contingent of professors who taught courses and advised students in the adult education study area, my primary interest. I decided I would minor in rural sociology, an area of study that had long interested me. Professor Burton Kreitlow agreed to be my major professor. He understood that I would be taking courses part-time—one or two a semester—since I was also teaching courses and assisting with extension staff development work. He told me that, according to graduate school rules, I would have to study full-time for one academic year. That meant taking leave from my teaching and extension position and receiving no salary for nine months. With no savings, house payments to make, and a wife and three children to feed and clothe, I continued to have some serious doubts about my new position.

5 Teacher and Student

Ruth and I decided that I would wait at least a year before taking a leave of absence to meet the graduate school's full-time study requirement. That would give us time to figure out how to meet our expenses while I had no income. Delaying would also allow me to complete several courses before taking leave and studying full-time. But we also knew that the more quickly I completed the degree, the sooner I would become eligible for the pay hike and promotion that were part of my agreement with Dean Pound.

Knowing very well the responsibilities I faced, Walter Bjoraker excused me from teaching a course in the spring of 1965—but he did assign me five master's degree advisees, all county extension workers who were on leave to complete their graduate degrees. (As part of Director Ahlgren's agreement with Dean Pound, if county staff were to receive salaries comparable to campus-based faculty and be treated as bona fide faculty, they had to at least have earned a master's degree.) As an advisor, it was my job to point the students toward the courses that would both fit their interests and meet the requirements of a master of science degree. Several of the courses were in our department: Evaluation of Extension Programs, Program Development, and Administration of Extension. Many other graduate-level courses were available throughout the College of Agriculture and other schools and colleges on campus. I had to hustle to stay one step ahead of my advisees by talking with other professors and reading course descriptions.

As part of my own course work, I enrolled in a required midlevel statistics course and found myself doing more remedial math than I expected. It was one of the most difficult courses I had taken in a long time, as math was never one of my great interests. Another requirement for the PhD degree was to have working knowledge of at least two foreign languages, so I enrolled in a late-afternoon French course, along with a couple hundred other PhD candidates from across campus. When I faced conjugating French verbs, I was completely lost. I had never even learned how to conjugate English verbs. I enlisted my niece, Janet Olson, who was attending high school at the time, to teach me how to conjugate English verbs, and soon I was on my way in the French course.

Every evening I locked myself in a bedroom in our little home and studied statistics. I enjoyed the challenge of both courses, but I despaired over not having more time to play with my three little kids, who often asked, "Where's Daddy?" I tried to devote an hour each evening to playing with the kids. Their favorite game in those days was "horse": I kneeled down, all three climbed on my back, and I shuffled around the living room.

By the end of the spring semester, I had passed the French language requirement and decided to study Spanish on my own. That summer I enrolled in a community development course taught by the Department

While teaching and doing extension work full-time, as well as taking graduate courses part-time, I had to make sure to set aside time to play with our three children, Sue, Steve, and Jeff.

of Rural Sociology, my PhD minor. It was an excellent course that got me thinking about many things I had not thought about before: the nature of rural communities, the relationship of villages to farms, and the characteristics of rural education. I was beginning to enjoy my PhD program, even though the pressure was still on to complete it so I could fully meet my job responsibilities and return to a more normal home life.

In the fall I studied advanced statistics and Spanish. I also worked on developing a proposal for a PhD dissertation research project and I taught my Introduction to Extension course. It was a very busy and demanding time.

I was so busy, in fact, that I did not have time to consider the unrest that was beginning to swirl around on campus and across the country. The United States was fully involved in the Vietnam War by the end of 1965, with 184,000 US troops in Vietnam. In April 1965, while I was busy studying French and statistics, twenty-nine faculty members and fifteen hundred students staged a teach-in on the UW–Madison campus to protest the war in Vietnam. On April 17, 1965, fifteen thousand students gathered in Washington, DC, to protest the war. On November 27, thirty-five thousand student protestors met in Washington and circled the White House.[1] More protests were coming, and I would soon be forced to take more notice.

Fred Harvey Harrington had become president of the University of Wisconsin on August 6, 1962, after the death of President Conrad Elvehjem. The University of Wisconsin, the Regents, and newly appointed President Harrington began examining a new organizational structure for the university. One of the most far-reaching and controversial changes was a proposed reorganization of Cooperative Extension and other outreach activities conducted by the Madison campus. Harrington, a former history professor, was a supporter of President Lyndon Johnson's various Great Society programs, particularly those designed to help the urban poor. Harrington was impressed with the successes of Cooperative Extension in rural communities and wanted to merge Cooperative Extension (based in the College of Agriculture) with General Extension (a freestanding outreach program based on the Madison campus but not part of any college or school). Harrington included WHA radio and television in the merger, creating a super-organization called University of Wisconsin–Extension, which would have its own chancellor, deans, and directors.

Dean Pound and many College of Agriculture faculty members opposed the merger, but the Regents approved it. Much of the Cooperative Extension budget and the director of Cooperative Extension would be pulled out of the College of Agriculture to become part of the new organization. On October 22, 1965, Harrington appointed Donald McNeil chancellor of the University of Wisconsin–Extension. The new organization included several divisions: Program and Staff Development, Liberal and Professional Studies, Economic and Environmental Development, Human Resource Development, Methods and Media, and Community Programs. A new office space in the Extension Building at 432 North Lake Street housed the new chancellor and other administrative offices, including Program and Staff Development, directed by my old grad school colleague Patrick Boyle. The staff development people in my Department of Agricultural and Extension Education would work out of two offices, one in Ag Hall, where they would advise students and teach campus courses, and one in the Extension Building, where they would conduct their new program and staff development activities, now considerably expanded to include all outreach faculty: Cooperative Extension staff, former General Extension staff, plus radio and TV staff.

From my perspective, it all seemed considerably clumsy—especially having two offices, which required that I walk the half-mile from one office to the other every day, sometimes twice a day. But I was about to go on study leave, so none of this would affect me until I returned to work in 1967.

In preparation for my study leave and a year without a salary, I applied for and received a two-thousand-dollar scholarship that UW–Extension offered for extension faculty seeking advanced study. I also applied for a student loan, something that was not common at the time for older returning students. The Dane County Department of Social Services had responsibility for interviewing students seeking student loans. I met with a very stern woman who asked me a series of questions. She began with: "Aren't you a little old to be going back to college?" (I was thirty-one.)

I said it was a requirement of my job. I tried to explain that I held a teaching position that required a PhD degree and I must earn a doctorate to keep it, receive a promotion, or expect any increase in salary. She scribbled some notes on a piece of paper without looking up.

"And why is it your parents aren't helping pay for your advanced schooling?"

"They are retired and living on a fixed income," I answered.

"Oh," she said, writing more notes on her yellow pad.

I left feeling not at all certain that I would receive the loan, but two weeks later I received a letter in the mail indicating that my loan had been approved. Ruth and I now had four thousand dollars for the coming year, plus a couple thousand more that I had saved. It was still only half of what my salary had been, however, and we knew that the next twelve months would be a financial challenge.

Now that I was on study leave, for the first time in nine years I did not go to my office on the first workday in January. I could spend some time with the kids, who were three, two, and one. I did have a desk on campus, first in a School of Education temporary building in a former residence on Johnson Street, and later at another former residence on University Avenue. Several graduate students in education shared the space, all from other parts of the country and the world. I was the only one who had a permanent residence in Madison.

For the first semester I carried a twelve-credit course load, full-time for a graduate student. I also worked hard on developing the research project for my dissertation, the culminating work for a PhD student. My courses included research strategies, an advanced adult education seminar, philosophy of education, and a history course. I had never taken a philosophy course and anticipated it with dread. Philosophy to me seemed an area filled with questions and authors who wrote thousands of words, hoping to find something to say. My major professor, Burton Kreitlow, suggested I might find the course interesting. Thinking back, I believe what he really thought was that my scientifically trained, "show me the evidence" mind would benefit from a course in philosophy. How right he was.

The course, with an emphasis on John Dewey's philosophy of education, was taught by College of Letters and Science professor William Hay. I found him to be considerably different in manner and dress from any agricultural professor I'd ever met. He wore pants and a shirt that looked slept in, tennis shoes, and no necktie. On the first day of class he declared, "I don't like how the author of your textbook has arranged the material in the book, so I tore out all the pages and rearranged them in a more proper order." He held a bundle of pages secured with a big rubber band. As he began lecturing, with the rubber band removed, stray pages dropped quietly to the floor.

I had never experienced anything like it in the many classes I had taken over the years, and on that first day of class I had great difficulty focusing on what he had to say. I was more interested in when the next page from his re-organized book would filter to the floor—and whether he would begin searching for any of the stray pages as his fifty-minute lecture continued.

He carried the sheaf of papers with him as he paced in front of us, occasionally reading a passage or two. Sometimes he leaned over a podium as he talked, star-ing at his room full of advanced graduate students (who by the second and third week were beginning to worry about the grade they might receive in the course and how it would be determined). Other times he walked to a cor-ner of the room and rested his head against the wall, with his eyes closed and no words coming from his mouth for a minute or two. Some of us thought he had gone to sleep and would eventually slide to the floor to continue his nap. But he was not asleep. He was thinking. And much to my surprise, he got me thinking as well, about such questions as: What is the nature of human nature? What is the essence of knowledge? What does *knowing* really mean? How do ethics and aesthetics apply to teaching and learning? What is a teacher's proper role: to pass on knowledge, to offer opportunities so students can learn on their own, to focus more on how-to-learn skills than on information to be memorized?

His teaching goal, I eventually figured out, was more about students developing their own philosophy of education than on memorizing the contributions of the classical education philosophers. He wanted us to develop a process for determining our own personal philosophies about learners, about knowledge, and perhaps most important of all, about the role of ethics and of aesthetics in education. I began to ponder the power of critical thinking, and why every educator, at any level, should both encourage it and practice it him- or herself. He got us thinking about three branches of philosophy: metaphysics (the theory of reality), epistemology (the theory of knowledge), and axiology (the theory of value), words that I had never used and knew little about. And to be frank, I initially considered these words the most esoteric and profoundly useless as anything I had ever encountered.

But by the end of the first semester of my study leave, I was having a grand time wrestling with an abundance of new ideas, learning how to do research, and applying all of that to my own research project. I had always been interested in leadership and, more specifically, leadership strategies—and this became the focus of my research as I attempted to relate young people's preferred leadership strategies to their socioeconomic status.

Ruth's and my social life, what little there was of it, focused on gatherings with other graduate students, most of whom had to be as frugal as we were. There were many "bring your own bottle" potluck suppers. It ended up being one of the most fun years our family had had in a long while. I had deadlines to meet, of course, but there was no travel and no sitting in never-ending committee meetings. There was an opportunity for reading, time for thinking, and perhaps most important of all, time to discuss ideas and perspectives with fellow graduate

students. It was during some of these discussions that I
learned the importance of understanding as fully as pos-
sible a perspective that I didn't agree with. I learned to
argue my own perspective with logic, with evidence, and
with passion—and without too much emotion, which can
cloud or even prevent critical thinking.

To earn a little extra money, I taught workshops
for the relatively new Volunteers in Service to America
(VISTA) program, which was part of President Lyndon
Johnson's Economic Development Act of 1964. The purpose of the program was to teach volunteers to work with
low-income and otherwise underprivileged people. In
the first VISTA workshop where I was to share principles
and teaching strategies for adult education, one of the
more outspoken members of the group challenged me.
She knew something about my work as an assistant professor at the university.

"Why should we listen to you when we all know that
the universities are in the pocket of the federal government's military-industrial complex?" she asked.

The question stopped me cold. I'd never been challenged in this way before, and I surely hadn't thought
that I was a part of any military-industrial complex. I
wasn't sure how to respond to her at the time, but I said,
"You decide if what I am offering in this workshop is of
value for the work you'll do in VISTA." She stayed in the
program. I learned as much from the VISTA volunteers
as they learned from me, especially about the issues the
country was facing at the time: the Vietnam War, civil
rights, environmental protection, and women's rights.
Working as a county extension agent and then in the
College of Agriculture, I had been somewhat insulated
from what was happening on other parts of campus. This

While on study leave in 1966, I taught workshops for participants in the Volunteers in Service to America program. *WHI IMAGE ID 61840*

would soon change, as student protests increased both in size and frequency.

With the Vietnam War raging and no end in sight, on May 16, 1966, some four hundred UW students staged a seventy-two-hour "draft sit-in" at the university's Administration Building. Police were on the scene but were ordered to stand down unless there was property damage or university officials were prevented from carrying out their duties. No police action was taken.[2]

I was busy on the other end of campus that day, but I heard about it from some of my fellow graduate students and read about it afterward. I was conflicted. I could understand students' opposition to being drafted into the military. But I was concerned about fairness. In 1965, I had completed ten years in the US Army Reserve and received an honorable discharge as captain. All the boys in my high school class had served in the military, and several of them had fought in Korea. No one wants to face combat, but history has proved that some of us must. My generation had done so; now it was this generation's turn, and they were protesting against it. I was not especially sympathetic to their cause.

During the fall semester, I completed gathering data for my research project and finished writing my dissertation, which I titled "Style of Leadership and Personal Characteristics Desired in Adult Leaders by Low Socio-Economic Rural Youth." Not the most exciting title, to be sure, but it was in the style of PhD dissertations written at the time. I had long been interested in leadership approaches, and I had a continuing interest in improving the plight of the rural poor. My research led me to useful insights on both topics.

Since my grade school days, I had been interested in writing, so as a break from my academic work in the fall of 1966 I enrolled in a noncredit course on freelance writing taught by Al Nelson, a full-time writer living in Delafield who taught part-time for UW–Extension. I already had considerable writing and editing experience, but I had never tried to have anything published outside of my work responsibilities. In this once-a-week, four-week class, Al taught me about query letters and proposals, about rejection letters and writing markets, and the value of keeping a journal. With all of my other responsibilities, I had been lax in keeping up with my journal writing. I vowed to correct that, and I did. I have been keeping a journal ever since.

I thoroughly enjoyed Al Nelson's workshop, in part because the style of writing he advocated was so dramatically different from my dissertation writing style—which was the approved academic writing style of the day: all third person, few active verbs, lots of footnotes. The workshop confirmed a goal I'd had since my county extension days; someday I wanted to pursue a career in freelance writing. But Al was upfront about the expected income for full-time writers. I quickly decided I'd better stick to my academic career and do freelance writing as a secondary endeavor.

To start, I pursued the idea of writing a freelance weekly newspaper column. That year I contacted Howard Sanstadt, editor of the *Waushara Argus* in Wautoma, the county where I grew up, and pitched him a column called *Outdoor Notebook*. My family had acquired an old run-down farm earlier that year, and I had already written several columns during breaks from dissertation writing about our experiences on our land: planting trees, the kids fishing in the pond, and other nature topics. Howard said he would run the column for a few weeks to see what reaction he got from readers. I would go on to write the column for ten years, 520 columns.

At the end of my year-long study leave, I received my PhD degree,
with a major in adult education and minor in rural sociology. Here
the children help me celebrate.

The top pay I earned was five dollars per column. Al
Nelson was right: Keep your day job, because freelance
writing doesn't pay well.

On a snowy day in November 1966, I defended my
dissertation with my five-member graduate committee.
I passed. I filed my dissertation with the graduate school
and breathed a huge sigh of relief. I had completed the
requirements for a PhD degree.

I attended the January 1967 UW graduation ceremony at the UW Field House. Following the festivities,
my brother Darrel and his wife, Marilyn, who lived in
a nearby apartment, held a reception for my immediate family and my major professor, Burton Kreitlow. My

parents, my brothers and their spouses, and of course Ruth and our three little kids attended. When I introduced Professor Kreitlow to my parents, he said to my mother, "You should be so proud that your son is now a doctor." My mother, who had not graduated from eighth grade and who was quite overwhelmed by all the pomp and circumstance of the event, said, "He's no doctor. He can't even cure a chicken." (For my mother, there were three kinds of doctors: medical doctors, dentists, and veterinarians.)

I never could have earned my PhD without Ruth's support throughout the process.

Later, my father shared with me a piece of wisdom that he often used when referring to well-educated people. "Just because you have a lot of education doesn't mean you know anything." My parents were obviously proud of my accomplishment, but they also valued being humble. I've never forgotten their comments.

6 Big Changes, Big Challenges

On January 2, 1967, after a year's study leave, I was back
on the payroll and at my desk with my newly minted
PhD degree. I was now eligible to advise graduate students pursuing their own PhDs. I also was placed on an
assortment of department committees. The University
of Wisconsin–Madison has a long tradition of faculty
governance, with faculty members serving on committees determining campus policy, new course approv-
als, tenure recommendations for faculty, and more. I
was appointed to my department's graduate admissions
committee, with the charge of deciding who was accepted as graduate students in the department, and the
curriculum committee, where I helped decide about new
courses and other curricular concerns.

   As I sat at my desk in Agriculture Hall, I thought about
the many changes that had occurred on campus since I
completed my master's degree in 1957. That year, campus enrollment during the spring term was 15,017. During the spring semester of 1967, student enrollment had
climbed to 25,591—an increase of 10,574 students in ten
years. Graduate student numbers increased even more
dramatically, from 2,764 in 1956–57 to 8,192 in 1966–67.[1]

One reason for this growth was the increase in research dollars coming to the university. Federally supported research at UW–Madison increased from $661,000 in 1950 to $8.87 million in 1960, from 15 percent of the university's research budget to 45 percent. The majority of the federal money came from the Atomic Energy Commission, the National Institutes of Health, and the National Science Foundation.[2]

With the increase in federal research dollars came ever more pressure on the faculty in all schools and colleges to write research proposals and conduct research activities. A major determinant for obtaining promotion and tenure was a substantial research program supported by outside financial resources and resulting in published journal articles. However, I had earned tenure in 1964 as an assistant professor, so this increased emphasis on research and publication had less effect on my academic career than it did on nontenured faculty members.

I had been promised promotion to associate professor with an increase in salary when I completed my doctorate, and Dean Pound, true to his word, recommended my promotion to associate professor on July 1, 1967, with a thousand-dollar increase in salary. For our family, the financial stresses lessened. But the country at large was being torn in many directions, with many stresses and challenges for its people.

The Civil Rights Act, signed by President Lyndon Johnson in 1964, created new opportunities for African Americans and women, but it led to serious pushback. In 1966, Betty Friedan's National Organization for Women began advocating for equal rights for women. That same year, race riots erupted in Milwaukee, Omaha, Chicago, Atlanta, and Lansing, Michigan. African Americans wanted their plight understood, and now with their rights ensured by law, they protested, often violently. Race riots continued into 1967.

At the same time, the escalating Vietnam War incited student protests, sit-ins, and strikes on campuses across the country. On April 4, 1967, Martin Luther King Jr. denounced the war in Vietnam, evoking an angry response from President Johnson. On April 14 in San Francisco, thousands marched to protest Johnson's policy in Vietnam. By the end of June 1967, US troop numbers in Vietnam reached 448,400. The country's nerves were raw. Many continued to support the war, believing it would stop the spread of communism. But more and more people, particularly college students, called for the war to end.

Adding to these feelings of unrest and uncertainty, thousands of people across the country were mobilizing to protect the environment, many of them prompted by Rachel Carson's 1962 book *Silent Spring*. The country was awash in protests, at the cusp of far-reaching change.

The year I was on study leave, I still was so busy attending classes, doing my research, and writing my doctoral dissertation that I had little time to become involved with these issues. I read the newspapers, and occasionally I sat in on a heated discussion with other graduate students, but that was about the extent of my awareness. In those days I didn't even think much about what was "liberal" and what was "conservative." I knew about the University of Wisconsin–Madison's long history of student protests, and in my travels while working for the state 4-H office I had talked with many people who were upset with the university's policies; some even told me that they would never send their son

SIFTING AND WINNOWING

During my years on the University of Wisconsin campus, I often walked past the famous "sifting and winnowing" bronze plaque fixed to the side of Bascom Hall. The quotation's roots trace to 1894, when a school official accused Professor Richard Ely of being a Socialist and supporting unions. The UW Board of Regents received a request to censure the professor; in response, on September 18, 1894, they approved the following statement:

> Whatever may be the limitations which trammel inquiry elsewhere, we believe that the great State University of Wisconsin should ever encourage that continual and fearless sifting and winnowing by which alone the truth may be found.

The class of 1910 presented the "Sifting and Winnowing" plaque to the university, but the Board of Regents rejected the gift with concerns it would encourage radicals to appear on campus. After a public outcry, the plaque was mounted on Bascom Hall in 1915, where it remains to this day. It reflects the value the University of Wisconsin places on individual intellectual and academic freedom. That value allowed me, and so many others, to explore areas of thought that were not considered mainstream at the time. It also encouraged me to push my students to think about new things and use new learning approaches.

or daughter to the UW because it was too big and too liberal. It wouldn't be long before I saw firsthand the strife on campus that had begun to upset many people in the state.

My appointment upon returning to work consisted of 25 percent teaching (in the College of Agricultural and Life Sciences) and 75 percent extension work (in the new University of Wisconsin–Extension).

For the spring semester of 1967, I returned to teaching my Introduction to Extension course. I also received permission from department chair Walt Bjoraker to offer a noncredit, informal graduate student seminar that I titled Developing a Working Philosophy of Adult Education, the first of its kind offered in the department.

Half a dozen graduate students enrolled in the seminar; I had taken classes with several of them when I was completing my PhD degree. For the seminar, I built on the educational philosophy course I had taken the year before while I was on study leave. Together the seminar students and I explored the application of philosophy to adult education. I knew how practical-minded most adult education teachers are, and I was concerned that my seminar would be a bust—that philosophy, with its far-ranging questions and esoteric answers, would be seen as frivolous and a waste of time. But that was not the case. Participants took the seminar seriously, and we had fascinating and productive discussions, many of them prompted by the student protests on campus, the riots occurring in major cities, and the general feeling that profound change was happening across the country and especially at the colleges and universities. We discussed the nature of change and what forces evoke change. We examined what we considered legitimate strategies for creating change, how quickly change should occur, obstacles to change, and the role educational institutions can and should play in creating, understanding, and adapting to change. We pushed for ever-deeper questions: what is the essence of human-kind, what's the difference between accumulating information and *knowing*, when should change be resisted and when should it be embraced, and what are the moral and ethical approaches to bringing about change? Perhaps most important of all, we explored the question of why educators need a personal philosophy of education—to know what they believe and the basis for those beliefs.

The seminar was one of the most interesting things I had done in my career, and at semester's end I knew that I must offer it again. It evolved into a three-credit course that I taught once or twice a year for twenty-eight years on the Madison campus and at other universities in the United States and Canada.

Our department always had several international graduate students enrolled, and on occasion we hosted international educators who had traveled to the UW and wanted to visit with our department's faculty. As I wrote in my journal,

> July 18, 1967. I spent the day with ten extension workers from Zambia discussing group dynamics. A highly motivated and eager to learn group. Their country is but three years old and they are interested in making their independence work.

That summer of 1967, I taught a four-week summer school course in leadership development, much of it based on my PhD research. Twelve students enrolled. I also contributed to decisions about graduate student progress, never easy to assess.

July 19, 1967. I serve on the graduate committee for a
PhD student from West Pakistan. He talks and talks and
writes and writes but he never says anything. His graduate committee, which I chair, met to discuss his dissertation research plans. He shared many pages of plans
that said little and require a great amount of revision.
I'm concerned he won't pass his preliminary examinations, which are scheduled for September. Professor
Douglah, also on his graduate committee, says this fellow doesn't know how to listen—one reason he never
seems to focus on what is critical. His graduate degree
future does not appear bright.

During the fall of 1967, I experienced firsthand the
turmoil that had been brewing on campus. With my
split appointment between the College of Agriculture
and UW–Extension, I made the trip between my two offices nearly daily. On October 18, 1967, as I neared the
Commerce Building across from Carillon Tower, I saw
a huge crowd of students gathered there. I remembered
that Dow Chemical Company job recruiters were visiting campus, set up in the Commerce Building, where the
business school was then located. Dow manufactured
the deadly chemicals napalm and Agent Orange, both
used by the American military in the Vietnam War.

I had seen many student protests in the past few
years, but this one seemed different. I quickly became
aware of a huge police presence, not merely UW campus police but a large contingent of Madison police as
well, most carrying billy clubs and wearing helmets with
facemasks. I heard yelling and screaming and saw students coming out of the Commerce Building with blood
streaming down their faces. The pungent smell of tear

gas hung in the air, an odor I quickly recognized from my army training. I felt helpless to do anything. I heard the screams of ambulances arriving to carry away the injured, and more sirens as additional police arrived. The crowd of onlookers grew ever larger. More student protestors gathered outside the building, yelling and screaming, but the police were more concerned about the students inside the Commerce Building.

I later learned that Madison campus Chancellor Sewall had called in the police, who used tear gas and clubs to clear protestors from the building and to protect Dow Chemical Company's recruitment efforts. The next day, October 19, students called a general strike, and more than three thousand of them rallied on Bascom Hill.

> October 22, 1967. Last Wednesday, October 18, we had one of the worst student riots in the history of the UW. About 1,000 students gathered to protest Dow Chemical's interviewing on campus. Dow contributed to the war effort and in the minds of many students are criminals. About 75 students and 20 or more police officers went to the hospital within an hour. There were many charges of police brutality. One student stunt was to cut down the US flag on Bascom Hall. They haven't found the culprit yet. The faculty met at the Union until 11:45 p.m. on Thursday and voted to support Chancellor Sewall's stand on the matter. About half of the faculty members supported the students' actions.

After the late-evening faculty meeting at Memorial Union, students lined up for a couple of blocks outside the building, holding hands to create a corridor through which the faculty had to walk. The students said noth-

Demonstrators clashed with police during the Dow riots in 1967.
WHI IMAGE ID 3780

ing—no yelling or jeering—in an eerie silent protest.
Faculty members were divided: some supported the student protests, while others felt it was the university administration's responsibility to maintain law and order
and keep the institution operating.

For the most part, people living outside of Madison
were opposed to the student protests and angry about
the riots. "Why can't that university control its students?" was a question I heard often as I traveled around
the state as part of my university responsibilities.

October 23, 1967. Another faculty meeting at 4:30 p.m.
today focusing on student riots and police brutality. The
meeting adjourned at 7:00 p.m. after voting to have the
University Committee appoint an ad hoc committee to
study the event. It was good the administration waited

The Bascom Hill rally was one of many student protests that erupted on the UW campus during the 1960s. *Courtesy of the UW–Madison Archives, #S09139*

until Monday. Much had obviously been done behind the scenes as the meeting went much more smoothly than the one last Thursday.

The Dow riots were some of the bloodiest confrontations UW–Madison had ever known, and they did much to coalesce the student protest movement on the UW campus. Many students who had been uncertain where they stood or not actively participating in protesting the war were swayed by the riots and the police brutality. They joined the protests by the hundreds. Things would get worse before they got better.

Teaching Philosophy of Education helped inform me about the deeper issues involving the war in Vietnam and why students were so angry about it. I found myself changing from someone who believed the student movement was ill conceived and doomed to failure to someone who believed their protesting could contribute to real societal change.

Meanwhile, my Department of Agricultural and Extension Education was experiencing its own struggles as the faculty debated the pros and cons of departmental reorganization. Even after the rather dramatic reorganization of extension and outreach programs on campus, my department was considering additional major changes of its own. The Department of Agricultural Education (now named Agricultural and Extension Education) was organized in 1907 with the purpose of preparing teachers of agriculture for the state's high schools, county agricultural schools, and normal schools. The discussion about a departmental reorganization had begun in 1964, but it had sputtered along. The idea did not sit well with several faculty members who preferred to leave things as they were. But with all the other changes happening at the university, including the radical reorganization of extension, it seemed that perhaps it was time to institute a new organizational scheme for the department as well.

Walter Bjoraker, now chairman of Agricultural and Extension Education, had been meeting with adult education and vocational education representatives Wilson Thiede and Russell Hosler, both in the Department of Curriculum and Instruction in the School of Education, plus a faculty member with adult education responsibilities from the Department of Home Economics Education and Extension in the School of Home Economics. The group's first step was to create an informal organization called the Joint Office for Study, Research, and Development in Adult Education and University Extension. It was a mouthful of a name, to be sure, but one that engaged all the various departments involved in adult education and outreach activities. The Joint Office, as we referred to it, even produced some stationery, but it really was only an informal organization.

One practical purpose of the Joint Office was to provide an efficient way of coordinating adult education–related course offerings and research programs. The office also provided a way for faculty members in the various departments to get to know one another better and move toward organizing a new, consolidated department. This would result in a broader range of credit courses offered and would make it easier for faculty to work together on joint research projects.

But the Vietnam War and student unrest hung like a cloud over everything taking place on campus in late 1967, including my department's discussion of reorganization. An unnamed US senator said of the nation's attitude at the end of that long year: "It's a tiredness, a frustration, an uneasiness. It's a war with no end in sight. It's a racial and urban problem with no end in sight. It's a fiscal problem with no end in sight. Maybe if we all get out of here, go home and listen to the people for a while, we'll come back with new hope and new ideas and new enthusiasm. But maybe we'll come back more discouraged than ever."[3]

7 Education and Social Change

My responsibilities in UW–Extension were to assist with the staff training and development of faculty for the entire extension organization—more than a thousand faculty members. Pat Boyle, director of the Division of Program and Staff Development and now my boss, asked me to chair the planning committee for UW–Extension's second faculty conference. Boyle had chaired the first faculty conference, in 1966; I had not attended, as I was on study leave. Boyle told me that the first conference, organized mainly so faculty from the three units could become better acquainted, had accomplished that purpose but had also resulted in many questions: Was the merger really necessary? What was to be gained through adding layers of bureaucracy? And why make major changes now, in the midst of all the turmoil facing the country?

Chairing the faculty conference planning committee proved to be a daunting, frustrating, and sometimes nearly impossible job. I was assigned two half-time graduate assistants—Myron Johnsrud from North Dakota and Betty Burwell, a Canadian—to help with planning and organizing the hundreds of details involved. Their expertise and assistance proved indispensable as the conference planning moved from ideas to specific programs and activities.

One of my first concerns was how much autonomy the planning committee would be given. I met with Don McNeil, the new chancellor of UW–Extension and a former history professor, whom I knew wanted the conference to focus on how extension should respond to social issues, especially race relations problems in Milwaukee. But Gale VandeBerg, dean of Economic and Environmental Development, had other ideas.

> July 24, 1967. Pat Boyle and I met with Gale VandeBerg in his new office in the Extension Building. We discussed what should be the rationale for the new University Extension organization and what we should emphasize during the faculty conference. He believes the concept of planning for total resource development is still current. I'm not convinced. I think we need to develop a new rationale, now that University Extension includes much more than Cooperative Extension.

Reflecting on all I had learned about the social unrest surrounding the Vietnam War and the civil rights movement, I tended to agree with Chancellor McNeil. Confronting social issues would be a challenge for the new organization, but perhaps programming on those topics would help bring the faculty together.

> July 28, 1967. Annual conference planning is beginning to come together. We'll try to present a program to the newly merged faculty describing University Extension programs as they relate to societal change.

August 2, 1967. I met with the overall planning committee for the Extension conference to share our thinking
about the program so far planned. They showed little interest and said things like "Looks good" and "Go ahead."

I quickly became concerned about the planning
committee's hands-off attitude toward the faculty conference. I had expected to have more debate about the
conference agenda. Were people too busy trying to adjust
to the new organizational structure and new responsibilities? Did they see planning for the conference as
merely another committee assignment that had to be
endured, but not taken seriously? Did some believe that
a faculty conference, no matter how well planned and
carried out, was a waste of time for busy people with a
full slate of educational programs to manage? I didn't
have the answers to those questions.

Racial unrest in Milwaukee continued into the summer of 1967. Milwaukee had become one of the most
segregated cities in the nation beginning after World
War II, after large numbers of African Americans moved
there in search of employment. By the mid-1960s, job
opportunities had faltered, poverty in the black community was rampant, and segregation was the norm. On July
30, 1967, the powder keg ignited and riots broke out in
Milwaukee. Mayor Henry Maier declared a state of emer-
gency and asked for the governor to send in the National
Guard. Four people died in the melee and fifteen hundred were arrested.[1] In my journal I wrote:

July 26, 1967. Racial violence continues in Detroit and
several other Michigan cities. Thirty-six have been
killed. Thousands injured. Millions of dollars of prop-

erty destroyed. But this is nothing compared to the losses to the Negro community and their drive for civil rights. Much progress has been made, but race riots do not encourage white support of the movement.

August 2, 1967. Milwaukee rioting continues. Civil rights marches get out of hand and result in looting. Sniper fire. Many buildings burning. Wisconsin National Guard troops there on standby.

Black people's concerns in Milwaukee seemed a timely and appropriate theme for the upcoming faculty conference—but could my tiny staff and the planning committee pull it off, especially when the committee seemed to care little if there even *was* an annual conference?

With public broadcasting now a function of University of Wisconsin–Extension, our planning committee decided to work with colleagues in public television to create a film examining racial unrest in Milwaukee. The film would be shown at the conference and would air at thirty viewing sessions around the state. I hired George Vukelich, a freelance writer and radio personality with WIBA in Madison, to write the script.

Around the same time, Father James Groppi, a white Catholic priest in Milwaukee, took up the cause of blacks in that city.

September 5, 1967. Newspapers continue with stories of Father Groppi, a Milwaukee priest, and his marches on behalf of Black people and their demands for open housing. He certainly is creating an awareness of the problem.

CENTER FOR ACTION ON POVERTY

Building on President Johnson's War on Poverty legislation of 1964, in 1966 UW–Extension chancellor Don McNeil created a Center for Action on Poverty that cut across Cooperative Extension and General Extension interests. Dorothy Davids, a Wisconsin Stockbridge-Munsee Nation educator and staff member of the center, said this about its work:

> It seems it was our goal to teach "grassroots" people how to create change in their own communities. It was a revolutionary idea that African-Americans, Latinos, American Indians, women, physically disabled, and elders actually had some ideas on how to improve their lives. It was quite a jolt and maybe a threat to the establishment when they discovered that the established institutions did not have all the answers. The Center's role was to facilitate both the power of the people with differences to speak up and the people with the power to help bring about change to listen. . . . We were different, and we were learning.[1]

Chancellor McNeil worked long hours trying to change the attitudes and practices of extension faculty, many of whom did not agree with this new approach to programming. He was roundly criticized by some faculty and by others who believed UW–Extension had no business working with social issue programming.

The Center for Action on Poverty opened the eyes of many to the fact that University of Wisconsin–Extension could collaborate effectively with a diversity of groups. Further, the center demonstrated an approach to teaching that started with people—with their problems and concerns—rather than the traditional "listen up, we have information that you need" academic approach.

NOTES
1. Jerry Apps, *The People Came First: A History of Cooperative Extension* (Madison: University of Wisconsin–Extension, 2002), 93–94.

To add first-person perspective to the documentary film we were creating, I was referred to an African American student in Milwaukee, who agreed to talk with me about the plight of black people in Milwaukee. After we met, I wrote the following:

September 27, 1967. As part of the program for the extension annual conference, I interviewed a University of Wisconsin–Milwaukee student who is one of Father Groppi's followers. I asked him about freedom. He answered, "What's freedom? Freedom is everything all the white men has got now that I ain't got. Everything, baby. He can live where he wants. He build up a thing in his head and say 'I want to be this' and he can be that. I can't be because, when I build up anything in my head, I got to say, 'Okay. Sure, that's what you want to be. Now how do you do that if you're a Black man?'"

"What's the answer to all these problems faced by Black people?" I asked.

"Black Power. Get together with my Black brothers and we all goin' to get together, poor Black cats, rich Black cats, middle class Black cats, cats who are wearing their hair long. We're all goin' to be united by one common thing. We're all Black. When we get together

we are going to speak as one unit, just like every other
minority group has done in America. We are goin' to
do it, too. If it means voting Black, we vote Black. If it
means killing white, we kill white."

It was one of the most difficult interviews I had ever
done. The young man's responses to my questions were
powerful and provocative. I wondered, how would the
extension faculty, many of them not ready or willing to
rock any boats, react to his statements?

The many meetings and many hours spent preparing the documentary and planning the annual conference—that sense of responsibility—solidified for me the
importance of an educational institution teaching about
social issues, including the topic of education for change.
The planning committee truly represented the new UW—
Extension organization, with members' reactions to
my interview ranging from "You can't include that" to
"Can you find more stories similar to this?" And with
that range of responses, I knew the conference would
be thought-provoking and worthwhile. Those of us who
supported social-issue educational programming were
risking alienating some of the faculty and perhaps creating a rift that would make it more difficult to create programing that cut across disciplinary lines. We knew we
had the support of the extension chancellor, but he was
new, and we didn't know if his support was enough.

When we showed the film at the conference, the audience reaction was mixed. That was understandable.
Extension faculty members were concerned about their
future, about their responsibilities, about the day-to-
day basics like where their office would be located and
where they would park. These personal matters had to

be dealt with before we could explore a major change in programming direction. Our Program and Staff Development unit would do more training about educational programming for social issues in 1968.

The mid-sixties cemented many of my beliefs about education being much more than facts and information transmitted from teacher to learner. I felt more strongly than ever that education could be and should be a force for change, including far-reaching social change. My experiences in those years, both in conference planning and in teaching a course on the philosophy of education, provided the foundation for much of my professional work to come.

October 24, 1967. I spoke at a district 4-H leader meeting at the YMCA today. The leaders were discussing change and were quite responsive to some of my ideas. One thing I stressed: we must help students learn how to think rather than what to think. For some people that is a radical idea, but not for these 4-H leaders. Perhaps some of those who weren't speaking up differed with what I had to say. But I was encouraged.

8 Unrest Grows

The Vietnam War raged on. Student protests continued at the University of Wisconsin and on campuses across the country. On February 22, 1967, twenty-five thousand US troops launched a major offensive on the Cambodian border, the largest so far in the war.

At the same time, the desegregation and civil rights movements continued, with violent confrontations and race riots in many major US cities. The country seemed to be tearing itself apart, and the universities were at the center of much of the turmoil. Despite the student protests, several faculty members, myself included, asked what the university could do to help ameliorate the situation, such as teaching special seminars and meeting informally with students to discuss their concerns. A considerable number of University of Wisconsin professors joined the students in their protests.

Several of us on the UW–Extension faculty, along with Chancellor McNeil, were asking what extension could do. With our mission to take the knowledge and expertise of the university to the far corners of the state—to practice the famous "Wisconsin Idea"—we thought it was an ideal time to provide educational programming that would help Wisconsin citizens understand the issues facing the country.

The Program and Staff Development Division had primary responsibility for training extension faculty. But the University of Wisconsin–Extension was still a new

President Lyndon Johnson came under increasing pressure as opposition to the war in Vietnam grew.

organization, and administrators and staff were spending untold hours fussing with organizational and administrative matters while cities burned and universities
were disrupted again and again with protests, marches,
and sit-ins. US public opinion had begun shifting; when
a Gallup poll asked whether it had been a mistake for the
United States to send troops to fight in Vietnam, the percentage of those answering "yes" rose from 24 percent
in August 1965 to 47 percent in October 1967. By August
1968, a majority of those polled by Gallup—53 percent—
were opposed to sending troops to Vietnam.[1]

Meanwhile, I attended meeting after meeting, working to sort out organizational problems.

February 19, 1968. I spent the afternoon meeting with
UW–Extension's Community Programs staff members.
Bob Dick is director under the new organizational
scheme. Bob could not get a word out of the district directors who supervise the extension agents working in
the counties. He wanted their thinking. He didn't get it.
In the evening most of that group plus some 4-H people
met at Bob Dick's home to discuss the role of the Department of Youth Development (4-H program), especially as to how that department is related to the district
directors. Much work remains to be done. There is still
a great deal of misunderstanding.

March 28, 1968. I drove to Wisconsin Dells this afternoon (Camp Upham Woods) for a meeting of my
department's staff. We're back to the old argument of
trying to determine the future direction for the department (Department of Agricultural and Extension
Education), what should be the component parts of the

department, and how we should be organized. Should the Wisconsin Idea Theater (Bob Gard's program) continue as a part of the department? Why do we spend so much time on questions of organization, and less time on doing something that, at least for me, seems more important—discussions of new courses that might speak to contemporary problems, for example?

At the same time, the UW–Madison faculty, still stunned by the Dow protests the previous fall, was holding many all-faculty meetings at the Memorial Union.

March 13, 1968. Faculty meeting from 7 to 11 p.m. We are discussing problems associated with job interviews on campus. One group of faculty wants to stop all interviews. Another wants them only off campus. A motion was finally passed that interviewing will continue on campus. This had been the recommendation of the campus University Committee.

Once more I am chairing the all-faculty annual conference; this next one is scheduled for early 1969. I am wondering if all the time spent planning an all-faculty conference is worth it. Are there other approaches for helping the faculty develop new ways of programming, especially educational programing related to social issues?

That spring, as popular opinion continued to move toward supporting an end to the war in Vietnam, President Johnson saw his poll numbers dropping. Then he surprised us all.

April 2, 1968. President Johnson dropped a bombshell and said he would not seek reelection.

Just two days following the president's surprise announcement, tragedy struck.

April 4, 1968. Dr. Martin Luther King, 39, was shot and killed this afternoon in Memphis, TN. He was the leader of the non-violent civil rights movement and a Nobel Prize winner. So far the assassin has not been captured. What will this do to the violent civil rights movement in this country? Is non-violence dead? I hope not, but I'm concerned. The Joey Bishop program on TV this evening is devoted to Martin Luther King. Wayne Newton sang "The Old Rugged Cross."

A writer for *Time* magazine wrote:

Rarely in American memory had hope and horror been so poignantly fused within a single week. . . . President Johnson's announcement of a major peace offensive in Asia . . . that the long agony of Vietnam might soon be ended. . . . [And] in Memphis, through the budding branches of trees surrounding a tawdry rooming house, a white sniper's bullet cut down Dr. Martin Luther King Jr., pre-eminent voice of the just aspirations and long-suffering patience of black America.[2]

The reaction to Dr. King's death was immediate, and devastating.

April 5, 1968. Fires in Chicago. Fires in Washington. Fires in Detroit. Rioting in Memphis, Raleigh, Tal-

lahassee and Nashville. Looting. The National Guard
called out in many states. Federal troops ringing the
White House. A machine gun positioned on the White
House lawn. Can't this society maintain its sanity?

10,000 students assembled for a memorial ser-
vice on Bascom Hill and then 15,000 marched down
State Street and around the Square. Will Martin Luther
King's death be marked by memorials like this univer-
sity event? Or are we witnessing the start of another
Civil War in this country?

The *Wisconsin State Journal*'s front page article read:

The Rev. Dr. Martin Luther King Jr., who carried the
dreams of millions of Negroes in his non-violence
battle for racial freedom, was slain by a white sniper
Thursday and violence erupted in the ghettoes of
America. Rioting broke out in Memphis, Raleigh, Tallahassee, and Nashville after King, 39, the 1964 Nobel
Peace Prize winner, fell dying on the balcony of his motel room, a gaping bullet wound in his neck.

There were disturbances in Harlem, Brooklyn,
Washington, and a dozen cities in the south.

"Martin is dead . . . God help us all," gasped a civil
rights leader when he heard the news.[3]

The next day, the *Wisconsin State Journal* reported
from the wire services:

Thousands of National Guard troops were sent into
action across the nation Friday to control Negro ma-
rauders who roamed city streets in a massive out-
break of violence and vandalism. President Johnson

sent federal troops into Washington. The toll of dead
climbed to at least 14 in the wave of arson, shootings,
rock-throwing, and looting triggered by the slaying of
Martin Luther King.

Five were dead in Washington, five in Chicago, and
one each in New York, Detroit, Minneapolis and Tallahassee, Fla. Hundreds of persons were injured, more
than 350 in Washington alone. More than 1,500 persons were arrested—at least 800 in Washington—as the
soldiers sought to stem the tide of violence.[4]

On the UW campus, students organized one of the
largest demonstrations in the history of the university.
From eight thousand to ten thousand University of Wisconsin students and faculty members and Madison residents, the vast majority of them white, marched from
Bascom Hill to the Capitol Square and then back to the
campus by way of Langdon Street.

Dennis Cassano of the *Wisconsin State Journal*
reported:

The somber group began its walk up State St. to the
Capitol at the conclusion of a militant memorial service for the assassinated Negro leader at the base of
Lincoln's statue on Bascom Hill. Chancellor William H.
Sewell began the service saying that white people have
to "heed to what is in the minds and hearts" of Negroes.
"Dr. King," Sewell said, "challenged the forces of ha-
tred and bigotry. This man, more than any other, gave
us hope that some day this nation might rise above rac-
ism and intolerance."[5]

In my journal I wrote,

April 7, 1968. Today has been proclaimed a National Day of Mourning for Martin Luther King. Services were held at the Capitol and at the First Congregational Church. Looting and rioting has subsided somewhat, but as several newscasters said on the evening news, "What will the white back-lash to the rioting and looting do to the Civil Rights Movement?"

April 21, 1968. The big social issues of the day appear to be: hippies, social dropouts, Vietnam War, Black power and the civil rights movement. Young people seem more aware of these issues than at any other time in our history.

Increasing numbers of students on the Madison campus became involved with these issues. In addition to protesting social injustice, some students might also have been reacting against how large the university had become. UW–Madison's *The Daily Cardinal* in 1965 had argued that there was a "direct line from the university's size to the rise in activism." Students were reacting to the "bigness of the university and transformation of higher education into a process of 'mass production.'"[6]

A counterculture among students emerged on campus. Many dressed outrageously; others let their hair grow long. Some embraced the use of marijuana, LSD, and other hallucinogenic drugs. As historian Matthew Levin has written, "The counterculture flourished in Madison just as it did in many parts of the country. Not all students used drugs, grew their hair long, or engaged in casual sex, but the counterculture embodied a rejection of established authority that paralleled the New Left in many ways."[7]

• • •

I was an active member of our church council in 1968, serving as chair of the adult education committee and then as president of the congregation. Many churches were attempting to respond to the turmoil facing the country, and I was ready to suggest my church become involved.

> May 6, 1968. Church council meeting tonight. The big issue: what should be our church's involvement in social issues and more specifically "the Negro problem," as some call it, which has come into particular focus since the assassination of Martin Luther King? After considerable discussion, we decided to emphasize helping the congregation be more informed. Someone suggested we invite a Negro seminary student that someone knew to be a Sunday morning speaker. The concern raised was: should he be invited to say a few words or give a full-blown sermon? And, should he stand in the pulpit or behind the lectern? Some members of the council are so traditional. They worry more about where someone should stand than the importance of having this man speak no matter where he stands. Others were concerned that having a Negro speak on a Sunday morning would be too much of a shock to the congregation. It's about time that our church begins to realize that the Black man's problems are everyone's problems.

A month later—just when it felt the country couldn't withstand yet another violent event after all the killing in Vietnam, killing on the streets, and the assassination of Martin Luther King Jr.—another calamitous event occurred.

June 5, 1968. Another shock last evening. After win-
ning the California primary election against Eugene
McCarthy, Bobby Kennedy was shot after leaving the
victory celebration. Two shots entered his head. The
assailant used a .22 cal. Iver Johnson pistol. At this
minute, 8:50 a.m., Kennedy is in surgery in a California hospital. His condition is listed as very critical. A
suspect has been caught; he was grabbed at the scene
by Kennedy workers. The suspect carried no identifi-
cation and refuses to give his name to authorities. This
country has gone mad.

June 6, 1968. Robert Kennedy died this morning. What
a tragedy for a family that has already had so much
tragedy.

Even though there was disagreement within our
church council, we moved forward with an invitation to
several black speakers.

June 9, 1968. Six Negroes, an adult, Lonnie Bunch,
and five teenagers, from Chicago's inner core visited
our church. Lonnie Bunch spoke at all three services.
He shared some of the problems that Black people face
today. In the afternoon, Mr. Bunch and the five teenagers were on a panel that I moderated. About 80 people from church attended. (He spoke from the podium,
and not from the pulpit—one of the compromises we
made in inviting Black people to speak.)

During the question and answer period, one
church member jumped up and said, "I worked to get
where I am, why can't you people work?" This started
an argument. A Negro member of our congregation [I

believe the only one at the time] answered, "We would work if we only had a chance. We're only asking for a chance." It was a very exciting meeting.

Few African Americans worked for University of Wisconsin–Extension in 1968. It seemed appropriate that my unit, Program and Staff Development, employ someone of color, especially someone who could help with programming on social issues.

June 25, 1968. We are considering hiring Sid Forbes, a Negro, in Program and Staff Development. I spent most of the afternoon with him, helping him become acquainted with University of Wisconsin–Extension and our Program and Staff Development Division. Looks like we can hire him for $13,500.

We hired Sid as a staff member to assist us in expanding our approach in programming for diverse groups.

We also began creating social issue programming for extension faculty in an effort to develop strategies for similar programming for a statewide audience.

July 11, 1968. Today our Program and Staff Development Division sponsored a "Problems in Black and White" conference for UW–Extension faculty. About 140 extension staff members attended. Dr. Bill Brazziel, a Negro educator from Virginia and a visiting professor on the UW campus this summer, spoke to the group. I believe the conference went well.

Just when it felt like the country couldn't withstand any more bad news, stunning events unfolded in Au-

gust 1968 at the Democratic presidential convention in
Chicago. With President Johnson now on the sidelines
after announcing he would not run for reelection, several Democratic presidential candidates had emerged,
including Vice President Hubert Humphrey, Senator
Eugene McCarthy, and Senator George McGovern. Anti-
war demonstrators disrupted the proceedings both inside and outside the convention hall, and the violence
escalated when Mayor Richard J. Daley, who ran Chicago
with a heavy hand, called out the Chicago police to sub-
due, arrest, and even club protestors.

> August 31, 1968. The Democratic Party Convention in
> Chicago this past week tore the party into three pieces
> and caused many Americans to question our system of
> selecting candidates for the presidency. Mayor Daley of
> Chicago ran the convention. Riots erupted during the
> convention by hippies and yippies (yippies are hippies
> interested in politics). [The nickname came from the
> counterculture group Youth International Party.] Many
> were arrested; many injuries when police used their
> clubs too freely.
>
> The McCarthy people at the convention felt they
> couldn't be heard—a charge well founded. After Hum-
> phrey and Musky were nominated, McCarthy felt he
> couldn't support them. So the party is torn apart over
> issues of law and order and Vietnam. A three-way split:
> The Wallace followers—pro law and order. The Mc-
> Carthy people—get out of Vietnam now. The Humphrey
> contingent—primarily supporters of President John-
> son and his policies.

Early in the summer, division director Patrick Boyle announced that he had accepted a teaching position at an Irish university and would be gone for a year. He asked me if I would serve as acting director of Program and Staff Development in his absence. Chancellor Mc-Neil had already given his approval. I hadn't decided if I wanted to pursue administration as a career goal, and this would be my chance to find out. From the grapevine, I had heard that I was probably a bit young (at thirty-four) to serve in a director or dean role, but this position would last for only a year, so no complaints came forth.

I looked forward to the opportunity, but I was more than a little anxious about how I would be accepted by the UW–Extension administrative group, all of whom were several years older than me, with more experience.

September 2, 1968. I begin my duties as acting director of Program and Staff Development as Director Patrick Boyle leaves for a year's teaching assignment in Ireland.

September 7, 1968. A busy first week as acting director—a position comparable to dean in the UW–Extension organization. Lots of administrative detail to keep me busy.

I soon discovered that administrators attend meetings, lots of meetings, meetings every day. And when I wasn't attending a meeting, I faced piles of paperwork: reports to file, letters to write. I was supervisor of our relatively small group of Program and Staff Development faculty, several of whom had split appointments with other colleges on campus, as I did. And I had my fall course to teach and my work with my church.

September 8, 1968. University of Wisconsin–Madison President Harrington spoke at our first fall series of adult education programs at church. 175 to 200 people attended. We filled Fellowship Hall. Harrington spoke about the size of the university and the new left. "The new left members are not communists," he said. "For the new left, communism is obsolete."

It was an important meeting. Although President Harrington didn't change everyone's mind about the student protestors on campus and the faculty who supported them, he did come off as a caring person.

Around that same time, one of my fellow council members—who was certain Communists were about to take over not only the university and the state but the entire country—accused me of being a Communist.

"All of you professors are Communists; we all know that," he stated matter-of-factly. I smiled and let it pass.

The UW–Extension administrative group, of which I was now a part, met monthly at locations around the state.

September 15, 1968. Last Tuesday and Wednesday I attended the Extension Administrative Committee meeting—deans and directors within the organization—at the Sterlingworth Motel in Elkhorn. The main issue discussed: how can the community programs faculty (the county-based agents) better relate to the other extension divisions? And how can the chancellor's office better relate to the deans and directors?

Important questions. Probably. But not nearly as important as how extension can help to solve some of problems that are tearing the state and the country apart.

Many Wisconsin citizens, especially those with conservative leanings, struggled to understand what was happening at the university—student protests, sit-ins, and even riots. Some grew to despise the hippies that seemed to be everywhere on the Madison campus. When extension staff traveled off campus for work, we drove a University of Wisconsin car—white with the words *University of Wisconsin* painted in a circle on each door. To us the circle looked like a bull's eye, especially when we encountered folks who wanted to vent their wrath toward the university. In one incident that spring, I stopped at a northern Wisconsin gas station on my way back from a meeting. The gas station attendant wouldn't accept my university-issued credit card. If I was going to get gas, I would have to pay for it myself. "I want nothing to do with that [string of cuss words] university," he told me. He went on to let me know what he thought of student protests and those "damn hippies." He couldn't imagine, he said, why any parent would send their kids to "that damn liberal university." I paid for the gas with my own credit card and went on my way.

The university's reputation didn't improve when the following story appeared in state newspapers.

October 6, 1968. The University is in the news again. The play "Peter Pan" was staged with several girls dancing in the nude. This has the entire community and the state in an uproar. This does not help the image of the UW.

Just as I was settling into my role as acting director of Program and Staff Development, in December 1968 Chancellor McNeil announced that he was leaving the UW for a position as chancellor for the Maine higher education system.

Now what? Chancellor McNeil had led the charge for UW–Extension's involvement in social issue programming. Many people hoped our new chancellor would be Henry Ahlgren, who had been director of Cooperative Extension under the old system and now served as assistant chancellor for field and support operations. With Henry at the helm, his longtime supporters surmised, we would go back to the old system, with Cooperative Extension returned to the College of Agricultural and Life Sciences, and General Extension and Radio/Television as free-standing units.

I liked Henry Ahlgren, and like many of my colleagues, I hoped that he would become the next chancellor. But I worried that some of the agricultural extension people would convince him to scuttle the new extension approaches that Chancellor McNeil had been championing, especially those related to social change. My worries were not justified, however, and it soon became clear that our newly appointed Chancellor Ahlgren agreed with those of us who saw our new UW–Extension structure as a foundation upon which we could expand our programing.

9   Student Strikes and More Protests

On December 21, 1968, at a time of great discord in this country, astronauts Frank Borman, James Lovell, and William Anders left earth's orbit, circled the moon and photographed it, and returned home safely—becoming the first to do so. The Apollo 8 mission was a positive moment for a country deep in the malaise of assassinations and war. A *Time* magazine writer declared, "The year's transcendent legacy may well be that in Christmas week 1968, the human race glimpsed not a new continent or a new colony, but a new age, one that will inevitably reshape man's view of himself and his destiny."[1]

I was five months into my role as acting director of Program and Staff Development for UW–Extension and beginning to feel like I knew what I was doing. I had realized that the social requirements of the role were challenging, however. About once a month, one of the deans or directors of UW–Extension held a cocktail party at his home, dressy affairs complete with a hired bartender. Ruth and I were just beginning to recover financially from my year of study leave, and we knew we could not host one of these rather lavish parties for high-ranking administrators and their wives (the deans and directors were all men at the time). But I knew we must attend, both to meet the social obligation and because many important decisions were made at these parties. One memorable time, we hired a babysitter, Ruth put on the new dress she had sewn, and we headed to a dean's house in Fitchburg, just south of Madison. Arriving at the home, we saw no cars in the driveway and no lights in the house. Were we early? It turned out we were late—a day late. The party had been held the previous evening. Upon returning home and checking my calendar, we confirmed my error. I never told any of the deans and directors why we missed the party. For the next party, I got the date, place, and time right—and Ruth had a chance to wear her new dress.

In addition to my numerous new duties, I once again chaired the annual faculty conference planning committee. This year, however, we had to replace the traditional three-day, face-to-face gathering with an alternative.

February 1, 1969. The abbreviated annual conference was held on Tuesday. With [Governor Warren Knowles's] freeze on all budgets, we decided not to hold our annual three-day event bringing in faculty from throughout the state. Dr. Paul Miller from North Carolina Extension was our featured speaker. We used the Educational Telephone Network so he was heard throughout the state. We also presented awards via ETN and long distance calls to Senator [Gaylord] Nelson in Washington and Thurman White in Norman, Oklahoma.

Later that month, on February 12, the Black Peoples Alliance on the Madison campus organized a strike to demand the university recruit more minority students and faculty and create a black studies department. The strike turned violent, and Governor Knowles called out the National Guard to keep the campus open.[2]

> February 12, 1969. Lincoln's birthday. Riots on campus again. The National Guard called out tonight. So far only six arrests. Issue is over demands of Black students. Many white militants are marching and making a mess of the situation. Most Black student demands are reasonable, but militants push it all out of perspective. Ironic those riots over Black student demands should take place on Lincoln's birthday.

> February 18, 1969. National Guard still on campus. But about half of them, or 900, have been sent home. Situation has cooled somewhat. Among other things, the Black students want a Black student center with full power to select the faculty who will staff the center. Request is outside the rules of the university.

The National Guard remained on campus until February 21. A student-faculty committee began meeting to discuss the black students' demands, and on March 3 the group received a "Report of the Committee on Studies and Instruction in Race Relations." This would lead to the creation of the Department of Afro-American Studies in 1970.[3]

Protests continued on other campuses around the country. On February 13, 1969, thirty-three students were arrested at a sit-in at the University of Massachusetts. On February 18, students seized a building and started a boycott at Howard University in Washington, DC. On February 24, students occupied the administration building at Penn State, and on February 27, police charged picket lines and clubbed and arrested Chicano leaders at the University of California–Berkeley.[4]

Meanwhile, on March 1, 1969, Henry Ahlgren began as the new chancellor of University of Wisconsin–Extension. Many former Cooperative Extension staff saw this as a new day, with hopes that Cooperative Extension would return to its "rightful place" in the College of Agricultural and Life Sciences (CALS), the new name for the college approved in 1967. Dean Glenn Pound of CALS was among those who hoped this would happen, as he had never agreed with the new organizational structure. The restructuring had wrested from him considerable control over not only Cooperative Extension programs but valuable budget dollars as well. Budget concerns affected all of us.

> March 18, 1969. I am busy learning how to build a budget for the Program and Staff Development Division. I must have P&SD budget prepared by April 1. I am working with a $173,000 base, which isn't great. Total budget allocations are short for all extension divisions, with state-wide budget cuts in the offing.

To add to the unrest in Madison, the Madison firefighters decided to go on strike.

> March 28, 1969. Firefighters on strike in Madison. First time in history. All schools closed. Public meetings cancelled. Issue is pay comparable to police. Present firefighters pay rate slightly lower.

Headlines in the March 29 *Wisconsin State Journal* read: "Strike Continues, Despite Court Ban. No Progress

Reported: Council Will Meet Today." The lead article continued:

> Madison firefighters' first strike in history continued Friday night, despite court action against it and city officials' attempts to end the walkout. At 10:30 p.m., separate talks were called off without progress. City bargainers and Mayor Otto Festge met with representatives of the Wisconsin Employment Relations Commission (WERC) in the mayor's office, while members of firefighters Local 311 held a separate session with their attorney, John Lawton, in a separate office.[5]

On March 30, two days after the strike began, an agreement was reached and firefighters returned to their stations.

In between administrative duties at UW–Extension, I managed to squeeze in time to lead my noncredit seminar examining philosophical questions related to the turmoil occurring in the country, especially on campuses. Several students attending the seminar asked when I might be offering the seminar for credit. I began trying to figure out a way to do that.

At such a somber time, I was pleased that our secretaries in Program and Staff Development continued to see a lighter side to life. April Fool's Day was a good day to do that. What they did, however, took us all by surprise.

> April 1, 1969. Office secretaries in fine form. I was given a number to call, as was the usual procedure. I got Dial-a-Devotion and a Bible verse. Harlan Copeland was asked to return a call from a Mr. Wolf. He got the Vilas Park Zoo.

•••

By April of 1969, the United States had 543,000 troops in Vietnam, the largest number yet, and a majority of the American populace who responded to a Gallup poll said it was a mistake to be in Vietnam.[6]

On April 9, student unrest at Harvard resulted in police being called in: thirty-seven protestors were injured and two hundred arrested. On April 22, the City College of New York closed because of student unrest. And on April 24, US B-52 bombers launched the most vicious attack yet against North Vietnam, provoking more protests.[7]

Also at this time, I found myself with another career opportunity. Robert Boyd, a professor of adult education in the Department of Curriculum and Instruction and a member of the Joint Office, became editor of the *Journal of Adult Education*, a national quarterly research journal for adult education professionals. Bob asked me if I would be interested in becoming book review editor for the journal. Once he explained the position to me, I gladly accepted—though I probably shouldn't have, as my administrative duties in University of Wisconsin–Extension were nearly overwhelming. I was also expected to keep up my resident teaching responsibilities on the Madison campus, and I was trying to establish myself as a freelance writer. At the time, I was writing a weekly column for four central Wisconsin newspapers, and I was working on a book based on those columns, which was due for publication in 1970. I had never been a book review editor, but my love for books wouldn't let me miss the opportunity.

May 2, 1969. I will become book [review] editor for the Journal of Adult Education published by the National Association of Adult Education on June 1. It's a quar-

terly publication with 5 to 8 book reviews in each issue.
It will take quite a bit of my limited time, but it should
be interesting.

To fulfill my book reviewing responsibilities, I contacted the librarian at Steenbock Library (the library for the College of Agricultural and Life Sciences) and asked for advice on selecting books for review. She said she would send me past editions of *Publisher's Weekly*, a trade magazine that offered listings and reviews of recently published books. Every week I scanned through the magazine, marking books that looked promising for adult educators, and then asked my secretary to request review copies from the publisher. When the books arrived, I sent letters off to prospective reviewers, people I knew from conferences and others who had recently reviewed books for the publication. When the reviews came back to me, I edited them and sent them over to Professor Boyd for inclusion in the journal. Not only did I enjoy selecting the books and editing the reviews, but I found I was keeping up to date with what was new in the field, something that had become difficult with my administrative duties taking up so much time.

To set a good example and at the same time "practice what we were preaching" with our workshops on how to involve minorities both as professionals in extension and in our programming, I hired an African American woman as our lead secretary in Program and Staff Development.

May 22, 1969. This week my new secretary, Beverly Cunningham, started work in the Staff Development office. She is the first Black secretary for the Division.

My teaching duties on campus now included advising undergraduate, master's, and PhD students. Myron Johnsrud, who had worked for me as I planned the second UW–Extension annual conference, completed his work that spring.

> June 9, 1969. I escorted my first PhD student, Myron Johnsrud, through graduation. He will return to North Dakota, where he will be director of staff development for North Dakota Cooperative Extension. A joke in the family: if a PhD student is so smart that he or she can receive a doctorate, why must the person have help walking across the stage during the graduation ceremony?

Myron worked in North Dakota for a short time and then was hired as director of the Federal Extension Service with the United States Department of Agriculture in Washington. I was very proud of him and what he had accomplished.

In the summer of 1969, I taught my regular four-week leadership course and looked forward to Pat Boyle's return in September when I could step down from the acting director position. By this time I had mostly decided that higher-level administrative jobs were not for me. In my biased estimation, far too much time was spent in meetings, trying to hash out program directions, fussing with organizational chart tweaking, and, alas, worrying far too much about who would get credit for some program that worked well. I remembered, not fondly, the many hours several of us spent drawing boxes and lines to create organizational charts showing where everyone fit within the organization. I would have much preferred to be working on a new book I was thinking about writing.

Upon Pat's return on September 20, Ruth reminded me that now I might have more time for our rapidly growing children; in 1969, the kids were seven, six, and five. I agreed. I also looked forward to fewer meetings, more time to spend with the students I advised, and more time to work on my teaching, freelance writing, and book review editing.

But then another opportunity came along. When Pat Boyle returned, the Irish university he had worked for wanted a replacement, and Pat recommended G. L. Carter, a professor in Ag and Extension Education and editor of the quarterly *Journal of Cooperative Extension*, which went to Cooperative Extension employees across the country. Shortly after I learned Carter was leaving for Ireland, I got a call from Dean VandeBerg in UW–Extension.

"Could I convince you to edit the *Journal of Cooperative Extension*?" he asked.

He went on to explain that he was on the national board of directors for the journal and in charge of finding someone to replace Carter. He also explained what the editor's job required and said that if I took this on, my duties in UW–Extension would be adjusted to require fewer workshops and less travel.

Ruth and I agreed that editing the journal and the resulting decrease in extension responsibilities would mean fewer committee meetings and administrative tasks, and no fancy cocktail parties. Dean VandeBerg had mentioned that I would have a staff consisting of a full-time copyeditor, a design person, and a part-time secretary, and that the journal's office would remain in Agriculture Hall, where it had been under G. L. Carter's term.

One downside of this new responsibility was that I had to give up my fun job as book review editor for the *Journal of Adult Education*. Instead, I would be the extension journal's book review editor as well as general editor.

The social and political crises surrounding the university continued. By the end of 1969, President Nixon was in the White House and the country's Vietnam strategy had changed significantly. Nixon had ordered 50,000 troops to be withdrawn by April 15, working toward 110,000 withdrawn by summer. As a *Time* magazine writer stated that December,

> The change in atmosphere [in the country] has been remarkably swift. White House aides concede that the protest movement was rapidly gaining momentum at the time of the nationwide Moratorium Day of October 15. The President's November 3 speech urging the "silent majority" to speak gave thrust to the counter protestors. Yet his defiant attitude toward anti-war demonstrators also energized the massive peace marches in Washington and San Francisco on November 15.[8]

At the time I wondered how President Nixon's policies would affect the university and our student body. I would soon find out.

10 Kent State and Sterling Hall

The beginning of 1970 saw more violent student protests on and around the University of Wisconsin campus. On January 2, protestors caused thirteen hundred dollars in damage to the Army Reserve Center on Park Street, and the next day they set off a firebomb that caused twenty thousand dollars in damage to the Red Gym on the UW campus. On January 4, the primate lab on campus was firebombed.[1] Public opinion continued shifting to a sense that it had been a mistake to send US troops to Vietnam. By May of 1970, 56 percent of US citizens polled were against the war.[2]

I was busy editing the *Journal of Cooperative Extension*, teaching my spring semester course, and advising several master's and PhD students. I spent most of each week in my Agriculture Hall office, where the *Journal* office was located, and a day or so a week in my Extension Building office.

I soon discovered that editing a national journal took more time than I had anticipated. Not only was I reading through piles of submitted manuscripts from extension professionals across the country, but I was also selecting books from publishers for review and reading research

The staff of the *Journal of Extension* (back row, left to right):
Barb Schwarz, design; Colleen Schuch, copyeditor; Cathy Youngs,
typist; (front) Jerry Apps, editor. *Courtesy of the UW–Madison
Archives, #S10274*

articles that I summarized in the journal. I was also encouraged, not only by my colleagues at the University of
Wisconsin but also by extension faculty across the country, to make changes to the journal. "It's too stuffy, too
academic, too hard to read, and apparently written for

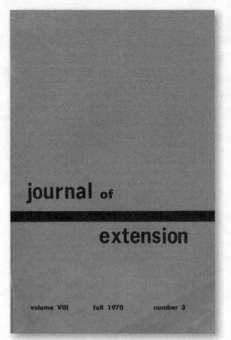

journal of

extension

volume VIII   fall 1970   number 3

Shortly after I became editor of the *Journal of Cooperative Extension*, we changed the name to the more broadly appealing *Journal of Extension*. I would be its editor for two years.

professors and administrators, not field staff." I heard these complaints time and time again. Others said the journal needed an updated appearance.

I felt caught between making some appealing but dramatic changes to the journal and risking alienating some of the longtime readers who liked the formal academic writing and the "serious" design of the publication. But Colleen Schuch, our copyeditor, strongly supported change, and Gale VandeBerg and Pat Boyle said they would support upgrades in the magazine.

I began by suggesting a name change. Since our state had recently combined Cooperative Extension and General Extension, I thought other states might be doing so as well, and I offered *Journal of Extension* as a title that might expand our readership beyond those who worked only for Cooperative Extension. Staff members Colleen and Barb worked with designers to create a new design for the cover, green with modern black type. Next we modernized the tone of the content by adding several new sections, including one called Points of View for which I urged contributors to take on controversial issues, such as extension's involvement in social issue programming.

Colleen, an experienced copyeditor, suggested we loosen up the writing with shorter sentences, first-person narratives, and the use of contractions. Of course, we got pushback. Some of our professor readers said we were ruining the journal, that it was no longer a scholarly publication. But we also received many positive comments, like, "Finally I can read the journal without becoming overwhelmed by the stuffy, academic writing!" By late spring I would write in my journal that our revamp of the *Journal of Extension* had been well received, and I predicted "great success for the coming year."

In February, General Electric was scheduled to recruit on campus. GE produced engines and weapons systems for the US Defense Department, and twenty-five hundred students marched from Library Mall to the Engineering Building to protest the company's presence on campus.

> February 12, 1970. Students protest against General Electric recruiting on campus. They marched, broke windows on and off campus, tipped over a police car. All is quiet tonight. Madison and Dane County Police on the scene to stop the melee.

One week later, February 19, more than a thousand students rampaged across the Madison campus, confronting police and breaking windows, in response to the conviction of the Chicago Seven, the group that had been arrested at the protests during the Democratic National Convention in Chicago in 1968.[3]

In March came a strike by the Madison campus teaching assistants. TAs served important roles in UW classrooms, leading discussion sections, helping professors administer and grade exams, and even on occasion teaching beginning-level courses. The strike would last for twenty-four days, until the Teaching Assistants Association accepted the university's offer of a contract that gave them recognition as a union with bargaining rights and more job security.[4]

> March 22, 1970. Teaching assistants (TAs) on strike this week. They claim too much teaching time, too little pay, and not enough say about what they teach. They have a point, but because TAs are state employees, the strike is illegal. This complicates the issue.

A few days earlier, on March 18, US Postal Service mail carriers went on strike in response to the federal government agreeing to a 41 percent increase in salary for members of Congress and a 4 percent raise for postal workers. Five days later, President Nixon announced on TV that he was calling up the military to restore "essential mail services" in New York City. By that time the mail strike had spread to one hundred cities involving more than two hundred thousand postal workers. The strike ended a week after it began.[5]

That spring, Senator Gaylord Nelson of Wisconsin seized on the protest energy to launch Earth Day. In a speech he gave at the UW campus Stock Pavilion on the eve of April 22, the first Earth Day, he said, "Earth Day is dramatic evidence of a broad new American concern that cuts across generations and ideologies. At last count, programs are planned at 2,000 colleges, [many] high schools and additional thousands of communities . . . involving young and old, liberal and conservative."[6] According to the Earth Day Network, "Twenty million Americans took to the streets, parks, and auditoriums that day to demonstrate for a healthy, sustainable environment in massive coast-to-coast rallies. Thousands of colleges and universities organized protests against the deterioration of the environment."[7] Earth Day 1970 marked a turning point in the environmental movement, and it helped establish Gaylord Nelson as an environmental hero. I considered myself very lucky to have had him provide the foreword to my first book, *The Land Still Lives*, published that same April.

Student protests on campus continued, but when tragedy struck at Kent State University on May 4, 1970, they escalated to an out-of-control riot. At a noon rally on the Kent State campus, Ohio National Guardsmen attempted to disperse the protestors. The crowd retaliated with shouts and projectiles. Guardsmen drew their weapons, several fired into the air or toward the ground, but some shot into the crowd, killing four and wounding nine students.[8]

The killings at Kent State triggered student strikes across the nation. The reaction on the Madison campus was swift. On May 5, UW students organized a rally for 7:30 p.m. The flyer announcing the rally, distributed widely, read in part, "US out of Indochina. Free all political prisoners. Shut down the University. Strike RALLY tonight." Once more the Wisconsin National Guard was called in. Unlike many campuses across the country, UW–Madison had stayed open and continued classes, even with a massive student strike in full force. On the west side of campus, students attended classes and sunbathed on the lawns, and the university baseball team played a regular league game with spectators filling the bleachers.

> May 6, 1970. It was a spring day of contrasts in Madison. A brief shower this morning followed by sunshine and cool temperatures. The crab apple tree blossoms on the mall leading to Ag. Hall are beginning to open. The tulips in front of the building are in full bloom.

> But it was also a day of turmoil. Last night the students voted to strike the university because of the Cambodian War decision made by President Nixon, and the Kent State shootings. As many as four thousand students attended the rally. Following the gathering, many of them went on a rampage, burning the Kroger store on University Avenue to the ground, starting a fire in King Hall and smashing all the windows in T-16 where the R.O.T.C. offices are located.

> I walked across campus after lunch today, toward State Street and smack into one of the confrontations of riot police with the protestors. As a result I got a healthy shot of tear gas and narrowly missed being hit by a rock-throwing protestor trying to pellet the riot police.

When someone asked me later how I responded to being caught between the police and the protestors, I responded, "I was no hero. I ran like hell."

Student protestors regularly targeted the ROTC offices located in a temporary building (known as T-16) left over from the years immediately following World

Protestors react to tear gas on the UW campus, May 1970. *Courtesy of the UW–Madison Archives, #031212 as 03*

War II, when student numbers escalated rapidly on campus. The building was only a hundred yards or so west of Agriculture Hall. I could easily see it from my office window, which faced west.

The student strike would last for nearly three weeks. Around noon each day, National Guard troops, with rifles in hand, surrounded the ROTC building. A few minutes later, a massive number of student protestors arrived, carrying stones, bricks, or whatever they could get their hands on. The students tossed stones at the National Guardsmen, and the Guard responding by hurling canisters of tear gas at the students. If there was a westerly breeze, as there was most days, the tear gas didn't stop at the students but curled up into Agriculture Hall and my office. Ag Hall had no air conditioning, so we kept the big windows open. Twice in one day I was teargassed in my own office.

After two or three days of what began to look like a carefully choreographed drama production involving the protestors and the National Guard, the dean's office in Ag Hall sent word to all departments in the building to gather up our most important records and bring them to his office, where they would be kept in a fire-proof safe. Upon reading the notice, one of my secretaries quit, saying the stress was just too much for her.

During those tense days, my graduate course on community development morphed into a discussion about how to protest nonviolently and, most importantly, without getting hurt or arrested. My students did not want to cross the student picket lines, which were in front of every classroom building, so we met in a meeting room in the back of the Methodist Church on University Avenue. The sessions were interesting and lively; instructions for active protesting for change did not appear in the standard community development literature. But in the estimation of my students and myself, protesting seemed like an effective way to bring about change. The class consisted of older students, many of them with spouses and children, and no one in the group wanted anything to do with violent demonstrations, the destruction of property, or the possibility of being injured or injuring others. But they agreed that the massive student protests on college campuses across the country were changing opinions about the war in Vietnam.

The distraction caused by the protests did not stop the normal progress of the school year, however. As graduation approached, my workload increased, and I began planning summer activities.

May 23, 1970. There are term papers to grade and PhD dissertations to review. Starting Tuesday morning, I've been getting up at 5:30 to read Laverne Forest's PhD dissertation. Laverne will graduate on June 8. We have hired him with a joint appointment with Program and Staff Development and with the Department of Agricultural and Extension Education. He begins work on July 1.

One of Laverne's future assignments will be to teach the "Introduction to Extension" course in our department, the one I taught since 1964. Program Evaluation has become increasingly important in Program and Staff Development. Laverne along with Sara Steele will have major responsibilities in this area. As tax dollars become tighter at every level of government, tax-supported programs such as Extension must be able to show that they are making a difference in communities and in the lives of people. Carefully constructed program evaluations can provide the detailed information that administrators need in making their case for continued tax support.

June 17, 1970. I have several major projects this summer: my summer course begins next week; I'll be teaching a course in leadership and group dynamics. I'm scheduled to give a major speech at an adult education conference in Milwaukee, and I must begin work on a professional book to keep up my publication record. (Part of my annual promotion and salary review is based on publications completed.)

Last Friday the University Regents met and approved promotions. I am now a full professor. Some faculty members responsible for making judgments about my promotion thought 35 was too young to be

One of my most enjoyable tasks as professor was advising students. Here Laverne Forest and I celebrate his PhD graduation with his two children and my three kids.

a full professor. Several others, especially Pat Boyle, thought otherwise and my promotion was approved. Being a full professor has its privileges: no longer do I have to think about what I do as helping or hindering a promotion. I make a contribution where a contribution is needed. I can say and write what I think (within my area of responsibility) and not fear that something said or written will affect my promotion. It's a good feeling. A bump in salary also helps.

On June 22, I noted in my journal that I had ridden my bike to work that morning—a four-and-a-half-mile trip that took about twenty-five minutes. It was the start of a habit I kept for the next twelve years, first commuting on a three-speed, then a five-speed, and finally a nifty ten-speed. I rode the city bus during the winter months. Commuting by bike or bus allowed Ruth and me to get by with one car and save money on parking and gas. Biking to work was not very common then, and there were no designated bike trails or lanes. Some drivers seemed to like seeing how close they could come to me as I pedaled along, and often they yelled at me to get off the road—roads were for cars. Only once in those twelve years was I hit by a car, and then neither the bike nor I was injured. The driver of the car was more distraught than I was, continuing to apologize and inquire of any injuries as I picked up my bike and pedaled on my way.

That summer I continued work on the speech I would give at the education conference in Milwaukee.

July 10, 1970. My talk is about fundamentals of adult education. I will stress three reasons why we must tackle fundamentals: (1) the aim of adult education is too narrow, (2) adult educators are often more concerned with means rather than with ends, (3) young people, because of changing values, will bring a new perspective to our adult education offerings.

July 19, 1970. I drove to Milwaukee last Thursday, to the UW–M campus where the adult education conference was held. Large crowd—more than 200. I believe my speech was well accepted. The speaker following me was from UW–M. He spoke to the group about how we all must learn to use more machines in our teaching

and that machines are the answer to many of the in-
structional problems in adult education. In one breath
he was talking as if people were an extension of a machine and later he said we must treat them as humans.
A talk filled with contradictions.

Throughout all the strife of the spring semester, the
University of Wisconsin–Madison managed to remain
open. As fall approached, I wondered again if the campus administration would close the university's doors.

August 22, 1970. The campus is quiet. There are many
rumors floating around about this fall. Some say the
university won't open, that the "crazies," as some of
the violent radical students are called, will start riots
during registration week. Some are predicting that the
students will have firearms this fall and there will be
bloodshed.

One of our former vice chancellors, Robert Atwell,
left to become president of California College. He was
quoted in the newspaper today saying that the Regents
and the administration at UW–Madison overreacted to
the riots and have used but one solution—bringing in
the police in large numbers. He suggested there should
be more discussion between administration and students to help squelch uprisings.

Fall will be interesting at the University of Wisconsin. The campus is beautiful now. How will it look in
mid-September?

An answer to my question came two days after I
wrote it.

August 24, 1970. Disaster on the UW–Madison campus
this morning. A bomb exploded in the Math research
center, which is in Sterling Hall, injuring three people
and killing a post-doctorate student in physics. We
felt the blast four miles away at our home on the west
side of Madison. It rattled our bedroom windows and
awakened me. When the radio news came on at 6:30,
I heard the details. The Math center is ruined, several
small fires started, a portion of the Sterling Hall wall
was blown out and every window in the building was
broken as were windows in the Chemistry Building,
which is next to Sterling Hall. Windows on the east end
of University Hospital, which is across the street, are
also blown out.

Is this the beginning of the student unrest this
fall? If so they've gone too far. Those students with legitimate concerns will never have a chance to express
themselves because of the backlash the bombing will
cause. There's an element within the protestor group
that wants the university closed down. These radicals
won't close the university, but the backlash from the
conservative taxpayers as represented by the legislature and the Regents will.

I'm concerned. What if the institution closed? I can
only think the worst. Tenure would mean nothing; we'd
all be out of work, and then what? Everyone would try to
sell his house and get out of the city—and no one would
be buying. If I were more pessimistic, I could go on. I
can't believe the university will close, but if this blast is
a sign of what's to come—well, it'll be hell this fall.

August 30, 1970. A busy, hectic week. The bombing last
Monday has everyone in a stir—what will be next? Will

A bomb set off by activists did devastating damage to Sterling Hall on the UW campus on August 24, 1970. *WHI IMAGE ID 33884*

it be Agriculture Hall? My secretaries are in a tither. The copyeditor for the *Journal of Extension* is moving her books and personal equipment home. She fears the worst. We are also making copies of many of our records, and I'm doing an inventory of my books in case they are lost.

The Math center blast loss is estimated between six and seven million dollars. Most of the old Chemistry Building was destroyed, as well as much of Pharmacy, and Sterling Hall. Windows were broken in all the surrounding buildings. The university has purchased nearly $4,000 worth of plywood to patch up the gaping holes left where there was once glass.

The F.B.I. has determined that the bomb was in a panel truck parked near the Math center. The truck was blown to pieces, but the F.B.I. is trying to put everything back together as they search for clues. The Regents have offered a reward of $100,000 for the bomber, all to be gotten from contributions. So far they've collected $25,000.

The editor of *Kaleidoscope*, an underground newspaper sold in Madison, reported that the bombing was done by the "New Year's Gang," a group of radicals that claim credit for trying to bomb the Badger Powder Plant near Baraboo the first of the year.

A university newsletter recounted the event:

At 3:42 a.m., August 24, a bomb of "unbelievable power" exploded in a loading dock at the east end of Sterling Hall housing the Mathematics Research Center, and physics, astronomy, and computing offices. One gifted researcher in physics, Robert E. Fassnacht, father of three, was killed. Two graduate students, a night watchman, and a hospital patient were injured. The lifework of five physics professors was ruined, as were PhD theses of two dozen graduate students who lost records, equipment, and research results. . . .

According to some, the big loss may well be the long-term psychological effect of the bombing on members of the affected departments. This was put into words by Philip E. Miles of mathematics: "Disruption appears to be a new way of life at the UW and our teachers feel this cannot go hand in hand with scholarship and teaching. Least affected by the outrage were the primary targets of the bomb, the mathematicians of the Math Research Center. Mathematicians work with paper, pencils, and immutable truth, all of which are relatively immune to bombs," he said.[9]

The death of a graduate student and the injury of four others created such an outrage among the citizens of Wisconsin, including most of the UW administrators and faculty, that violent protests skidded to a halt while law enforcement searched for the perpetrators. They were eventually identified as brothers Karleton and Dwight Armstrong, David Fine, and Leo Burt. Three of the four were caught and eventually served prison time; Leo Burt disappeared.

The university administration was doing its best to help faculty and staff cope with the tragedy, sending the following memo to all campuses: "Working with undergraduates involves opposing violence and destruction, but it does not mean 'holding students down.' Quite the contrary. It means joining students in effecting necessary and desirable change. It means moving forward toward the understanding, the cooperation, and the reforms that we need today and will need tomorrow."[10] The memo was signed by university president Fred Harvey Harrington.

Despite the bombing, the campus opened for classes that fall. I once again taught Introduction to Extension Education, for twenty-four students. I also worked on moving my informal seminar on educational philosophy toward legitimacy with a regular seminar number (981) and three credits. I would offer it with the new number and credits beginning with the spring 1971 semester.

Our department continued to wrangle over whether to join with others in the School of Education, the School of Family Resources and Consumer Sciences, and the College of Agricultural and Life Sciences to create a new cross-college and cross-schools department. One compromise all departments agreed to was letting faculty keep their current budget home, so there would be no transfer of budget from one administrative unit to another. The new department, if approved, would report to the deans of all three colleges: Leo Walsh (CALS), John Palmer (ED), and Hamilton McCubben (FRCS). Those faculty with partial extension appointments would also report to UW–Extension. On the surface it looked like an administrative nightmare, especially for whomever would be departmental chair—and would therefore report to three deans plus extension, and attend meetings called by any of the four administrative entities.

Nevertheless, it seemed more and more likely that the merger would happen.

September 27, 1970. Last Thursday and Friday I attended a retreat for the Department of Agricultural and Extension Education at St. Benedict's Center on the north side of Lake Mendota. The Dept. went on record favoring a merger with the other adult education units on campus. It'll be interesting to see if the merger will occur—we've been talking about it for six years.

With Henry Ahlgren at the helm as the new chancellor of University of Wisconsin–Extension, many old-time staffers were still hoping that the merger creating UW–Extension might be untangled and that all faculty and staff would return to their old administrative homes. In the end, the new structure remained in place, but several other organizational changes happened, including the creation of a dean of urban affairs position. Four statewide programs were combined into three divisions: Professional and Human Development, Economic and Environmental Development, and Educational Communications.

My duties as editor of the *Journal of Extension* continued. I looked forward to meeting with the publications committee in Washington, DC, in November. I'd already heard from a few readers that they felt the recent changes to its look and content were dramatic—but I didn't know if that was a compliment or a complaint.

November 15, 1970. From Monday to Wednesday I was in Washington, D.C., attending the National Association of State Universities and Land Grant Colleges' meeting, and the board meeting for the *Journal of Extension*. The board accepted my previously planned resignation to take place on June 30, 1971. I had set this date to resign when I accepted the assignment. The meetings went well. The group, nearly to a person, applauded our efforts to make the *Journal* more relevant to field staff, including the new sections we added. They applauded our attempts to avoid more traditional academic writing. They also liked the new cover design and the overall improved appearance of the publication. They knew I was due to leave behind my editorial duties after a two-year stint, but I was encouraged to continue editing the publication beyond 1971. I argued that it was good for a professional journal to have new blood at the helm every few years—and they generally agreed with me.

In December, Ruth and I invited my students and their spouses and friends to our house for a holiday open house. With twenty-one in my class, plus my graduate student advisees, it was a cozy but crowded affair. Ruth made a Christmas tree ornament to give to each student. We also invited everyone to join our family in decorating our Christmas tree; Vic Gidley, a PhD student from Australia and the tallest in the group, was able to put the star on the top of the tree with no difficulty. It was an interesting education for all—for my students, some of whom were from non-Christian countries, and for our children, excited to meet and share with this diverse group.

The party was a fun way to end what had been a tumultuous year.

December 31, 1970. And so the year ends. Nineteen seventy was a rich year for us. The children are all in good health and doing well and growing so quickly. The two highlights for me for the year were the publication of *The Land Still Lives*, my first book, and being promoted to full professor. My salary is now $19,311.

There have been some hectic times on the university campus in 1970. . . . But now the campus is quiet and students seem to be seriously pursuing their degrees.

11 Some Normalcy Returns

I looked forward to 1971 with some trepidation, unsure that I could handle another year like 1970. A feeling of uncertainty hung like a black cloud over the university. There was a clear possibility that UW–Madison might be forced to close. But on the positive side, I worked with a highly motivated group of students who were interested in change and willing to try various means of obtaining it. They didn't want to talk about the university closing, and neither did I. Students attended classes, professors taught, and the midterm graduation took place as usual.

The campus began to feel a little like it had before the student protests that had erupted during the 1960s. I hoped with some optimism that the faculty, the students, and the administration—the entire university—had, from the experiences of the past several years, learned about the meaning of change and the various ways by which it can be achieved.

January 31, 1971. Yesterday was graduation at the UW. Jack Powers, one of my PhD students, graduated and I escorted him across the stage. After the ceremony, Jack, his wife, Lea, and their five children, plus Jack's father, his brother and wife, and their two children were at our home for a celebration dinner.

February 10, 1971. South Vietnamese troops transported by American helicopters invaded Laos Monday creating quite a stir around the country. Most people want the war to stop and the Americans to come home. They see this invasion, although no American troops are involved, as a further extension of the war. The radical element of the University of Wisconsin–Madison student body prevented a faculty meeting from coming off as planned on Monday by shouting down President Weaver, who was selected as president in 1970 and took office in 1971. There was a rally about the war, with a march down State Street last night with the accompanying window-breaking. There has been none of this since last May. Now the Laos invasion triggers the unrest again. It's a good thing the weather is cold. It's hard to carry out a revolution when you're freezing.

March 6, 1971, I'm not teaching a regular course, only my philosophy seminar this semester, so I have more time for writing. I've just completed an article for the *Journal of Higher Education* on why graduate students have difficulty writing about their research. I'm also toying with an idea for a book providing a starting place for critical thinking. It's my feeling that far too many people these days want quick, easy answers to complicated questions, failing to realize the complex nature of the problem and its often multiple dimensions. I've started focusing on critical-thinking techniques in my philosophy seminar. I may try to develop a book proposal on the subject—it's more of an idea than a subject.

In June, the publications committee for the *Journal of Extension* arrived in Madison for a three-day meeting. They came from Colorado, North Carolina, Nebraska, Mississippi, Washington, DC, West Virginia, Wyoming, Michigan, and Milwaukee. Ruth and I invited the group, plus UW–Extension administrators Pat Boyle and Gale VandeBerg, for a cookout at our home. When it started to pour, we moved the two picnic tables into our screened porch and had a wonderful time talking, eating, and sitting elbow to elbow while we watched the rain fall. Several of them told me later that they couldn't remember when they had more fun at a picnic.

Meanwhile, national events continued to affect my work at the university. On August 15, 1971, President Richard Nixon ordered a freeze on all prices and wages in the United States. The action negated the salary increase faculty members were supposed to receive on July 1, 1971.[1]

August 20, 1971. President Nixon imposed a price-wage freeze in the country for 90 days. It began on August 15. The next day the stock market took its greatest leap upward in its history with a great flurry of trading. Nixon also imposed a 10 percent duty on all imports to help boost production in this country. As a result of the freeze, I'll lose the salary merit increase I would have gotten July 1. Had the Wisconsin legislature acted on the two-year budget promptly, we'd have gotten our raises.

September 19, 1971. The university opened last Monday, routinely and quietly. Not the anxiety we've felt the past two or three years. I'm teaching two classes this fall, 24 students in Intro to University Extension and

12 in my philosophy seminar. I'm experimenting with
a team-teaching approach for *Introduction to University
Extension*. I asked Pat Boyle and Laverne Forest to teach
principles of program planning, Sara Steele to teach
evaluation strategies, Robert Clark to teach administration, and I'll teach teaching-learning approaches
and extension history.

In an attempt to save tax dollars and "effect greater
efficiencies," several state politicians, including Governor Patrick Lucey, began looking for ways to reorganize
the university system. People both inside and outside
of the university lined up on either side of the issue.
Governor Lucey said he wouldn't sign the state's 1971
budget bill unless it contained provisions for merg-
ing the state's two higher education systems: the University of Wisconsin universities and the former state
teacher's colleges.

The University of Wisconsin was created by the state
constitution and state law in 1848. In 1971, it consisted of
the original land-grant university at Madison (founded
in 1848), UW–Milwaukee (reorganized in 1956), UW–
Green Bay (1968), and UW–Parkside (1968), plus ten
freshman-sophomore centers (now colleges) and statewide UW–Extension.

The Wisconsin State University system had its origins in an 1857 state law, which created a Board of Regents for Normal Schools. The first of nine such institutions opened at Platteville in 1866 and the last at Eau
Claire in 1916. In 1927, the normal schools received
authority to grant baccalaureate degrees in education
and were renamed State Teachers Colleges. With the
addition of liberal arts programs in 1951, they became

LAND-GRANT UNIVERSITIES

Sponsored by US Senator Justin Morrill of Vermont, the Morrill Act establishing land-grant universities was passed by Congress and signed into law by President Abraham Lincoln on July 2, 1862. For the first time in the nation's history, Congress had allocated federal dollars for higher education. The legislation read in part: "An act donating public lands to the several states and territories, which may provide colleges for the benefit of agriculture and the mechanic arts." In addition to providing the nation with well-trained agriculture workers and engineers, land-grant universities were required to offer military training, which led to the establishment of the Reserve Officer Training Corps, or ROTC.

In the 1860s, the federal government owned many acres of land. The Morrill Act stated that the federal government should grant each state thirty thousand acres of public land for each representative and senator the state had in Congress. States sold the land and used the money to establish a national system of state colleges and universities. In Wisconsin, where the University of Wisconsin had been established in 1848, the federal land grant helped to expand the university's offerings in agriculture and mechanic arts (engineering), providing money for constructing buildings, developing research farms, and hiring additional teaching staff.

NOTES
Morrill Act (1862), Ourdocuments.gov, http://www.ourdocuments.gov;
Editors of the Encyclopedia Britannica, "Land-Grant Universities,"
http://www.britannica.com/topic/land-grant-university.

Wisconsin State Colleges. In 1964, the Wisconsin State Colleges were designated Wisconsin State Universities.

The merger language proposed by Governor Lucey passed the state legislature, creating a new University of Wisconsin System on October 11, 1971, and combining the two public college and university systems under a single Board of Regents. Neither of the systems was in favor of the merger, and it passed, after long debate, by a margin of one vote in the senate. The law created a system with thirteen universities, fourteen (thirteen today) freshman-sophomore centers (now called colleges), and a statewide extension with offices in all seventy-two counties. Each university and two-year college was named "University of Wisconsin–" followed by the location or name.[2]

In the midst of all this reorganizational turmoil, I was offered a new opportunity.

December 4, 1971. The first week in November I flew to Los Angeles to attend the Commission of Professors of Adult Education annual meeting. To my surprise, I was elected chairman of the group. I flew to LA in a 747 airliner, a monster plane that held 350 people. There were only a few more than 100 on my flight so we had plenty of room. The plane seats eight people across with two aisles. The ceiling is high enough so you can stand up in front of your seat. We flew over Pikes Peak and the Grand Canyon, which were both pointed out to us by the pilot.

Upon returning home I learned that Pat Boyle presented the plan we had discussed to the Program and Staff Development staff that I will be sharing the administrative duties within the division. About half of the staff will report to me. It's an experiment and we'll see how it goes. Several staff members don't seem all that pleased with the idea. I will be associate director.

• • •

As we turned our calendars to 1972, my department continued to struggle with plans for consolidation and reorganization. Slowly I became more comfortable working as associate director for Program and Staff Development (75 percent of my time, with the other piece taken up by teaching). From my experience as acting director for one year, I had learned I could do administrative work, but I also discovered I didn't like it nearly as much as I liked teaching, researching, and writing.

As a reflection of the calm of the beginning of the new year, I wrote in my journal:

January 1, 1972. Today it's quiet on the block. Ruth and I didn't do anything last night except watch the Guy Lombardo show on television. I believe the announcer said it was the 43rd consecutive year that Lombardo welcomed in the new year with his orchestra. Our New Year's treat to each other was sleeping in, me until nine and Ruth until ten. I am usually up at 5:30 and leave for the office by 7:00. The first hour at work is the most productive for me, before everyone else arrives.

Major world events continued to unfold rapidly in 1972. President Nixon made a surprise eight-day visit to China in February, breaking down a standoff with that Communist country that had lasted for years.[3] Troops continued coming home from Vietnam. On January 1, 1972, the US military reduced its presence in Vietnam to 156,800. In June, five burglars were arrested for breaking into the Democratic National Committee offices at the Watergate Building in DC, setting off the Watergate scandal.[4] Peace negotiations with Vietnam began in October, struggled through the fall, and then collapsed in December, resulting in the United States carrying out more bombing.

My department, at a glacial pace, continued to discuss reorganization. By the 1970s, our department was seeing an increasing number of older students returning to the university for graduate degrees. Many were county extension workers who had been hired with bachelor's degrees and were now seeking master's degrees. Some of our staff members had difficulty adjusting to these older, experienced students, some of whom were older than their professors.

> January 5, 1973. Doris, one of my undergraduate advisees, stopped by the office today—in tears. She'd gotten a D from [Professor X] who teaches an introductory course she was required to take. [Professor X] is an old-time professor who believes that students are in class to have knowledge poured into their heads, and that he, as the instructor, should rule with a heavy hand. I've had numerous complaints from the students I advise about [Professor X]. But my problem is how to help [Professor X] see that students, especially older returning students, have considerable knowledge to share. And they often ask their professors difficult, sometimes challenging questions. These students should be treated with respect.

One of our up-and-coming young faculty members, Mohammad Douglah, who had grown up in Iraq, decided to move back to Baghdad to help care for his aging parents. His departure left a gigantic hole in the teaching/research program in our department, but it also opened up an opportunity for me.

January 5, 1973. Yesterday we held a reception for Professor Mohammad (Mike) Douglah in the office. He is leaving for Baghdad to be with his family. We'll all miss Mike and his family. He is one of the outstanding professors in our department, with the ability to think beyond the superficial problems. I am considering applying for his position, which means I would leave UW–Extension and work full time in my department, in the College of Agricultural and Life Sciences. I will not know if I can make the shift until July 1.

January 9, 1974. This is registration week, and business has been brisk as students return to the campus for the spring semester. I'll be teaching two courses this semester, one titled "Issues in Adult and Extension Education," and the other, which I will teach on the Richland Center Campus, titled, "Preparing Volunteers to Teach."

I am trying to adjust my workload now that Mike Douglah has left campus. For several years, I've been working a split appointment, approximately 75 percent of my time in UW–Extension (Program and Staff Development) and the remaining percentage in the department now with a new name (Continuing and Vocational Education) and a new organizational structure. It took ten years of discussion, but the new merged department will finally come into being on July 1. My goal is to work full time in the department. A search committee has been formed to find a replacement for Mike. With the split appointment, I find myself trying to do two jobs, and neither of them as well as I would like, in my judgment. I'd like to concentrate my efforts more than I have. I'd also like to begin a more extensive research program and do more writing. Much of my work in Program and Staff Development has been in administration, which takes so much time.

January 13, 1974. I met with Dean Pound about moving full time into the department. He agreed that it made sense to do so, but it was up to the department to decide. Now I must wait.

Professor Douglah's position was advertised nationally. Several candidates from around the country applied, as did I. Three of us were interviewed. I was selected.

After seventeen years with a full- or part-time appointment with Cooperative Extension, on July 1, 1974, for the first time, I would be a full-time teacher-researcher at the University of Wisconsin–Madison in the newly organized Department of Continuing and Vocational Education (CAVE). I left behind my appointment with University of Wisconsin–Extension, but I did not leave behind the Wisconsin Idea. I would still be responsible for various outreach activities, helping to take the work of the University of Wisconsin–Madison to the far corners of the state and well beyond.

My outreach activities would fall into four categories: providing on-campus noncredit workshops, teaching my philosophy credit course at other universities, giving talks at meetings and conventions, and serving as a consultant to colleges and universities interested in improving their on- and off-campus programs for adult learners and strengthening their research/outreach programs.

But I most looked forward to doing more hands-on teaching. For me one of the joys of teaching is how much I learn from doing it: new ideas, new ways of thinking about old ideas, the excitement of seeing a light come on in a student when something complicated becomes clear. For me teaching is more than passing on what I know to someone and then having that person regurgitate it back to me on an examination. Content transfer, as that approach is sometimes called, is merely the beginning of the learning process, for knowing is much deeper than collecting facts and assorted hunks of information. Facts are important. But ideas, feelings, and the ability to think and act in new ways are more important. It is my long-standing belief that as a teacher I should provide the setting for learning, an environment that challenges students but also provides a safe place to explore, make mistakes, examine old values and beliefs, and try on new ones.

12   Teaching, Research, and Writing

In late June 1974, I moved out of my office on the sixth floor of the Extension Building. Now I would be based entirely in my Agriculture Hall office. I looked forward to not having to maintain two offices.

The faculty and secretarial staff for our newly organized and expanded department, however, were located in three buildings on campus: Agriculture Hall, Home Economics, and Teacher Education. One of the compromises in organizing the new department was that faculty from the various affiliated schools would maintain their budgets in their home school or college—and would keep their offices in that school or college's building. My "budget home" was the College of Agricultural and Life Sciences, so my office stayed in Agriculture Hall, where it had been since 1962.

I appreciated the returning students in our department. Most of them had returned to school to work on graduate degrees after extensive work experience. They were older than most of the undergraduates on campus, most from age thirty-five to fifty. Many of them were teachers, some at vocational-technical schools, others for adult education agencies such as extension, and some with ten or more years' experience since their undergraduate work. A few were nurses who worked as staff instructors for a hospital or other health care organization, and several were responsible for adult education programs in museums and libraries. A considerable number came from other countries where they were responsible for an array of adult education programs, from community development to health care.

All were serious and hardworking. They knew the ways of the world, and they raised questions and made comments from their own experience that not only kept me and our other professors sharp but also added a practical dimension to many of our class discussions.

Most of these returning students had families and continued to work while they studied part-time. For some of them, finishing their degree program quickly and "getting on with their lives" was the goal, and this was evident by their actions and comments. For these few, this meant they wanted to do only the minimum requirements to complete the degree. But I saw the graduate school experience, no matter if part-time or full-time, as an opportunity to broaden and deepen perspectives, hone critical- and creative- thinking skills, learn how to conduct and interpret research and reach conclusions, and much more. This meant exploring well outside one's area of professional interest, as well as exploring in depth within a professional area.

The department established a weekend master's degree program as another response to the large number of older returning students in the late 1970s. It took some doing to get the graduate school's approval, as administrators there questioned whether a weekend, part-time program would have the rigor of full-time study in

One of the great gifts of student advising was getting to know, and learn from, graduate students from around the world. Here I am meeting with PhD candidate Vic Gidley from Australia.

residence on campus. But the program was well received both in Wisconsin and nationally and continued to thrive into the 1980s.

January 23, 1981. Tonight I met with the weekend adult education philosophy class for the first time. We will meet five weekends between now and May. We met from five until nine on Friday evening, with an hour off for supper. Then tomorrow, Saturday, we will meet from eight in the morning until three in the afternoon. Many out-of-town and out-of-state students have enrolled in

CRITICAL THINKING

A long-range goal for my teaching is to help students learn the importance of critical thinking and develop the skills for doing it. The day is long past when teaching was a matter of merely passing on information to a room of note-taking students looking forward to the next exam, when they will regurgitate what they have memorized. Gathering information is just the beginning of the learning process. Helping students develop their critical-thinking skills takes learning to a broader and deeper level.

The process of critical thinking is straightforward, yet some of my students struggled with it. Here is how I explained the process.

Critical thinking usually begins with a *question*—for example, "Is climate change real?"

The second phase involves consulting a variety of sources, reflecting on one's own experience, listening to authorities on the matter, observing what others are doing in this area of inquiry, trying something and recording its success or failure, and listening to a colleague who has experience similar to yours. For the question about climate change, a student would search the Internet and consult the library for research studies on climate change, read books on the topic, perhaps interview a climate researcher, maybe even travel to a place where glaciers have been receding, such as Alaska. The student would also read what climate change deniers have written and said about climate change.

A danger at this point in the critical-thinking process is latching onto the first reasonable-sounding answer to the question. I encourage students to look beyond that first good answer—to consider it an entry point as they search for additional answers. Critical thinking means being critical of *all* the ideas (or answers) we uncover and examining them from multiple perspectives.

Often during the process of gathering information, students will discover viewpoints, ways of doing things, or ideas that run counter to what they have long believed. This can be very uncomfortable for some learners—but it is an essential part of the process. At this stage of critical thinking, a person's confrontation with long-held beliefs can lead to discarding old beliefs and accepting new ones.

One of the challenges for teachers is maintaining the patience to allow students to wrestle with the challenges that result from critical thinking. In my experience, the students who struggle the most with the process are those who go into it believing it is irrelevant or unnecessary, those whose minds are already made up. Critical thinking becomes especially difficult for students who begin to uncover answers to questions that are clearly in opposition to their long-held beliefs. A student considering the question of whether climate change is real might already believe the concept is impossible, or a hoax. But upon examining the evidence from multiple perspectives, including viewing the effects of climate change firsthand, the student, through the process of critical thinking, reexamines the question and decides that strong evidence supports the existence of climate change.

this program. Several of our regular full-time students prefer the flexibility of the weekend format and have enrolled as well.

January 26, 1981. Reflecting on the weekend course. I have 20 enrolled, just the right size for many of the things I do in class. One student is from London, Ontario, which is farthest away. Many of the students are mid-career people who are working on a graduate degree in order to find another job.

In addition to the returning students from the United States, our department had always attracted international students from several African countries, from Israel and Iraq, from Japan and Thailand, from Sweden and Mexico, and other countries. They added a rich diversity of experience and cultural background to our classes, but not without some challenges.

Adnan Makli, one of my PhD advisees from Baghdad, Iraq, planned to return as a professor of extension at the University of Baghdad upon completing his degree. When Adnan arrived, he didn't speak enough English to carry on a conversation. He brought with him a translator when we met for the first time. But he was bright, and he learned English quickly—with a few lingering language differences. When he told me about a particularly long-winded professor he'd had for one of his early courses on campus, he told me, "My pencil didn't stop until the last word he spoke."

Another Iraqi student, Amand, stopped by my office early in the semester.

"Professor Apps, I need your advice," he said.

"I'll help if I can," I said.

"You are probably wondering why I don't talk much in class."

"Yes, I sometimes wonder why you're so quiet."

He became very serious then and began recounting something that had occurred the first time the class met. During the break, a US student had said to him, "Why have you been speaking? Your English is so bad that none of us can understand you."

Amand stopped talking for a moment. He stroked his black beard and then looked right at me.

"Professor Apps," he said. "I . . . I am very sensitive." And then the tears began flowing.

After a time he composed himself and told me that he had a part in a presentation his class group was responsible for during the next class period. He asked if he should go through with it. I was so angry I could hardly contain myself. I wanted to sit down the student who commented on Amand's English and say, "Listen, damn you, we're trying to build a learning community here, and a community is often made up of diversity. You might learn something from someone who speaks English a little differently than you do."

Amand wanted my assurance to go ahead. He also wanted to learn how to pronounce certain words such as Phi Delta Kappa. Together we went over his list of words. He listened intently to my pronunciations as I tried to control my anger over what he had told me. The next day, he did extremely well in his group's presentation. I suspect he practiced saying the words correctly for hours. What a terrible injustice students sometimes do to each other.

The more time I spent doing hands-on teaching, the more I learned about effective ways to introduce my students to critical and creative thinking. In my lectures, I told stories, most of which came from my experiences going back to my childhood on the farm and my early days as a county extension agent. I also created a variety of exercises designed to make the usual, unusual; the ordinary, extraordinary; the common, uncommon. I had my students draw pictures, construct models with Legos, and listen to music as ways of helping them think about things they hadn't thought about before and seek information from sources they hadn't thought of exploring.

Some students in my graduate courses didn't appreciate my teaching approaches, especially those that on the surface didn't appear to be directly related to the subject at hand. After the second session of one semester-long course, a tall, blond man in his early thirties stood up, looked me in the eye, and asked, "When are you going to teach me something? I mean, really teach something? I've had it with your questions and stories and silly exercises." I bit my tongue and tried not to sound defensive. I told him, "Hang with it for a while, and you might be surprised."

"I hope so," he answered.

During the break, I noticed that a couple of other students were talking with the young man who had doubts about my teaching approach. They had taken other classes of mine; I assumed they were encouraging him to stay open to the process. At the next class session, the fellow seemed more settled and accepting.

In my Philosophy of Adult Education course, I found journal writing to be a powerful tool. I asked students to keep a journal for the duration of the course, writing whatever they wished—thoughts about what they were learning, what they found confusing, questions they

I used a variety of approaches to help my students learn critical and creative thinking skills. *Courtesy of the UW–Madison Archives, #S10345*

had, or anything else. I told them I was a longtime journal writer and explained that often when I began writing about something I didn't understand, the process of writing helped clarify what didn't make sense to me.

I went on to say—as several of my more pragmatic students rolled their eyes—that journal writing can create new ideas and insights, lead to new solutions to problems, and help the writer clarify his or her personal values. I explained that keeping a journal creates a historical record. For instance, at the end of a course a student could go back and review the history of his progress in the course, what he learned and what concepts he struggled with, and so on. The journal could provide a learning record—a kind of blueprint for the learning that had occurred. Finally, I said that the process of writing in a journal can be a trigger for creativity itself—a way to tap into one's subconscious.

One student was quite skeptical of my lecture on the benefits and mysteries of journal writing. Yet the next time the class met, she told me that when she reluctantly began writing in her journal, she found that words began to appear on paper, words that she "did not know from whence they came," as she explained. I told her that's what tapping into the subconscious is all about. It's as if there is a conduit from the brain through your arm to your pen and then on to paper.

As I began each class session, I asked those students who were comfortable doing so to share something they had written. This sharing helped me as the instructor to know how the class was progressing, and when students heard others sharing similar reflections and questions, it helped them feel that they were not alone. I learned invaluable lessons teaching that Philosophy of Adult Education course, and my experiences with those students provided the content for my first professional book, *Toward a Working Philosophy of Adult Education*, which was published by Syracuse University in 1973.

After I was promoted to full professor on July 1, 1970, in addition to my teaching and outreach responsibilities I was expected to conduct research and publish my findings. Some new professors, especially some who had previously been secondary school teachers, had difficulty adjusting to the fact that now not only were they expected to be exemplary teachers, but they must also manage a research and publication program. A few professors I knew were good teachers and researchers but were not especially good writers and didn't embrace the "publish or perish" requirement.

I was lucky in that I enjoyed both writing and doing research. I had developed my interest in writing as a direct result of my experience with polio at age twelve, when I couldn't participate in sports and other physical activities. And I had loved research since I was a little kid and curious about almost everything, constantly asking, "How does this work?" "Why did this happen?" "Where did that come from?" In my undergraduate work at UW–Madison I had learned the basics of scientific research, but it wasn't until my master's degree program that I found the type of research I truly enjoyed: social science research, which required that I do research directly with people rather than in a laboratory. I was hooked.

My career-long research work at UW–Madison eventually focused on three areas of interest: leadership, older students returning for university degrees, and the foundations of adult education. I had been interested in leadership since the years I served as a 4-H club junior leader (I once won the state outstanding junior leadership award, which included an Elgin watch with a 4-H clover on its face), and I did my PhD research project and dissertation on effective adult leadership among the rural poor. My interest in adult education grew out of my own experience returning to the classroom in 1965 at age thirty-one to earn my PhD degree.

Finding outside funding to support research was (and continues to be) a challenge for university faculty. I struggled for several years with little financing for my research, but then something interesting happened. I had been an active member of the Adult Education Association (later renamed American Association of Adult and Continuing Education) since 1967, and in 1976 I chaired the association's publication committee. One of our responsibilities was to select a publisher for the 1980

Adult Education Handbook, the group's annual publication. Two publishers had submitted proposals, McGraw-
Hill of New York and Jossey-Bass of San Francisco, and
I arranged to meet with a representative of each on the
campus of the University of Chicago. During my meeting with company owner Allen Jossey-Bass, he let me
know that he wasn't happy that he had to fly clear out to
Chicago to be in competition with McGraw-Hill, a newcomer to adult and continuing education publications. I
interviewed the McGraw-Hill editor, Robert Manley, as
well, and after considerable discussion, the publications
committee awarded the 1980 adult education handbook
contract to Jossey-Bass.

A couple of days after the Chicago meeting, Manley
called me.

"Would you be interested in working part-time for
McGraw-Hill as an acquisitions editor in our college division?" he asked.

For a moment I said nothing. I thought he had been
going to express his anger with me for not awarding
McGraw-Hill the contract. I regained my senses and
asked, "What would be involved in the job?"

"We'd like you to help us establish an adult and continuing education unit within our College Division and
help acquire some manuscripts for the division."

After more discussion, I realized that this new connection might lead to a publishing outlet for my own research and might even be a source of funding. I agreed to
do the job. I would work part-time for McGraw-Hill for
seven years.

13 Department Chair

When our Continuing and Vocational Education department was three years old, in 1977, the faculty elected
me department chair. In those days, chair was not a
position that most faculty members wanted. For those
interested in working their way up the administrative
ladder, chairing a department was a logical step toward
becoming an assistant dean, then an associate dean, and
perhaps someday a dean. But most faculty members in
my department and others on campus were quite happy
teaching, doing outreach work, and conducting research
and writing. They weren't interested in stepping on the
treadmill of administration with the hope of achieving
higher-level administrative positions. Yet faculty members also knew that they must take their turn in the role
of department chair, especially in departments where no
one really wanted the job.

Usually a department chair served from two to five
years. Only tenured faculty members—associate and
full professors—were eligible. Chairing a department
meant constant personnel problems to solve, unending
committee meetings to attend, and slim budgets to

balance. Despite those drawbacks, the chair position became a career for some who liked doing the job and did it well.

Faculty governance came into play when selecting a department chair. Even though most faculty members did not want the job, they insisted on the right to vote on who would assume the role. At UW–Madison in those days, after the vote was taken, the results were submitted for approval to the dean of the college to which the department belonged. I do not know of a single time when the dean disagreed with the faculty's vote. Occasionally a dean might suggest a faculty member whom he or she believed would make a good department chair. But the dean could not appoint anyone without the faculty's involvement.

Chair elections in my department were run the opposite of how one would expect. Rather than having candidates state why they wanted to be chair and what they would do to improve the department, almost every candidate offered two or more reasons as why they *should not be elected*. Professor Kreitlow, one of our older, more seasoned professors, generally had the best negative platform. I remember during one election he claimed to have a statement from his doctor saying that if he became chair it would have a profound negative effect on his heart. (He seemed perfectly healthy to me.) We all knew that he would much prefer to concentrate on his teaching, writing, and research—which was how most of us felt. But his negative campaigning worked. Someone else was always elected department chair.

When I was elected chair in 1977, I didn't want the job. After serving as acting director of UW–Extension Program and Staff Development in 1968 and 1969, I had pretty much made up my mind that higher education administrative positions were not for me. But I couldn't come up with a convincing negative election campaign, and besides, as my colleagues pointed out, it was my turn. I was forty-three and had been in the department since 1964, full-time since the department's reorganization in 1974. My teaching and research-publication program was in reasonably good shape.

On my first day on the job as chair, I thought back to my first experience in a management role. The day after I turned eighteen, in 1952, I became manager of the H.J. Heinz cucumber salting station in Wild Rose. It was a seasonal job, beginning in late July and continuing until about Labor Day. My job was to supervise the staff, four men and one woman, who sorted and salted cucumbers. They swore a lot, complained even more, and worked hard—and surely wondered why Heinz had selected a kid to supervise them. I would have been lost without Monica Etheridge, who worked in the office, managing payroll, writing the checks for growers bringing cucumbers to the station for sale, and handling the complicated equations for how much salt to mix with how many gallons of water for a given number of cucumbers in the fermentation tank. Monica did all the brainwork while I tried to keep the crew of workers working. I had to fire one man, a drinker, because I was afraid he might fall into a pickle vat and drown. I also had to prevent two workers, both my age, from fighting with each other every chance they got. The hours were long: we opened at 8:00 a.m. and worked until the last cucumber was sorted and dumped into a tank, which on many days wasn't until 1:00 or 2:00 a.m. We worked seven days a week; the only time off was when it rained and cucumbers couldn't be picked. Monica and I were paid $1.25 an hour, while the rest of the crew earned $1.00 an hour.

In the four summers I worked at the salting station, I learned a lot about leadership, supervision, and administration. And I learned about people. I listened to and tried to calm down the occasional disgruntled farmer who brought in cucumbers and complained that we did not sort them properly and thus his check was less than he thought it should be. I got to know the hundreds of migrant workers who hauled the efforts of their day's work to the salting station. I learned to respect these men and their families. Most of them lived in southern Texas in the winter. They worked hard but enjoyed life. I had my first drink of tequila—which tasted a lot like kerosene—and I learned a passable bit of Spanish and better-than-average vocabulary of Mexican cuss words.

Would chairing a university be different from supervising the operation of a cucumber salting station? I was about to find out.

August 1977. I was scheduled to begin my duties as departmental chair on July 1, but I begged off for six weeks to complete a book I was doing for McGraw-Hill—*Study Skills for Those Adults Returning to School*. I moved my office from Agriculture Hall to the Teacher Education Building on Mills Street. A couple of weeks after I arrived, Mary Volkman, our departmental secretary, went into the hospital for surgery. I brought my secretary from Ag Hall, Nancy Trager, to the departmental office to temporarily replace Mary. Together we tried to keep the department going. Neither of us knew much about what we were doing. We filled out reports, appointed faculty to committees, and muddled along. During the first few weeks on the job, three secretaries left (we had 12) and they had to be replaced.

•••

As department chair, I would spend untold hours with our department's assistant professors, encouraging, helping, and evaluating their work as they pursued tenure—a complicated, time-consuming, even overwhelming procedure. After completing six years of work as an assistant professor, the candidate put together an extensive report of teaching, outreach, and research activities, including such evidence as student evaluations of teaching, reports from outreach activities, and copies of juried research reports that appeared in journals or books. This report was submitted to the department's personnel committee of elected tenured professors—the department chair plus four others. The personnel committee voted, and then, if the vote was positive, the department's entire tenured faculty voted. The tenure report, along with the department's vote and recommendations, were then submitted to a campus-wide committee. The committee reviewed and discussed the reports, voted, and sent their vote and recommendation to the dean of the college where the assistant professor was budgeted. The dean could accept or reject the recommendation.

In addition to working with my own department's assistant professors in their quest for tenure, in 1978 I was one of the twelve members of the Social Studies Division Executive Committee making decisions about assistant professor tenure promotions in other departments.

April 3, 1978. We had two Social Studies Executive Committee meetings this past month. We are the elected 12 who decide which social studies assistant professors should receive tenure. If a professor from another institution is hired by the Madison campus, we also consider his or her tenure at the time of hiring.

The committee has an onerous task, for it determines the career direction of all assistant professors in the social studies area (additional divisional committees on the Madison campus include: Physical Sciences, Biological Sciences, and Arts and Humanities).

In most cases, the decision to promote rests on the quality and quantity of research and published scholarship the person has completed. In some ways, the tenure-promotion by peers system is a monster. A newly hired PhD assistant professor is often so busy figuring out how to be a teacher, that it is easy to let research and scholarship plans slide. A big mistake.

The entire tenure system can be debated for its strengths and weaknesses. On the negative side, some assistant professors are so intent on producing juried articles that they lose sight of the reality of what they are doing. Some do not ask such basic questions as where, how and to whom does my research make a contribution? What is the relationship of my research to conceptual and theory development? In other words, how does my research relate to something else rather than stand as an isolated piece of work? Somehow the tenure review system hasn't communicated back to departments the need for assistant professors to work toward becoming thoughtful as well as being productive.

On the plus side, everyone promoted is carefully considered by his or her peers. This system over the years has resulted in an exceedingly strong faculty at the University of Wisconsin–Madison.

Chairing the department required untold hours of paperwork, with many reports, letters, and budget matters to consider.

• • •

I served as department chair from 1977 to 1979. The four deans I reported to told me I probably should have served longer. But after two years in the role, I wanted to concentrate on what I loved and knew best: teaching, research, and writing. I had decided I would rather work with students and with ideas than with the day-to-day problems a department chair had to face.

I had continued my research and writing during my stint as chair, and my first book with McGraw-Hill came out in 1978. For *Study Skills for Those Adults Returning to School*, I drew on my own experiences returning to school, I interviewed returning students, and I examined the study skill literature that had been published for traditional students (those coming to higher education directly from high school). The book included such topics as "Learning How to Learn," "Taking Notes, Listening, and Taking Examinations," "Improve Your Reading Ability," "Improve Your Thinking Ability," and "Become a Better Writer." Much to my surprise, the book sold thousands of copies.

In addition to researching the needs of returning students, I spent a considerable amount of research time examining how higher education institutions could provide a more congenial environment for older returning students, many of them wanting to study part-time as they continued working. In 1979, McGraw-Hill published my book *Problems in Continuing Education*, in which I discussed such topics as "How the curriculum should be adjusted for returning students" and "How teaching and learning approaches should be changed to accommodate older students." The book was well received in the United States, and translated editions were published in Spain and Jordan.

Problems in Continuing Education was one of several books I wrote reporting on my "adults returning to college" research project.

My outreach work continued as well, and I began teaching Philosophy of Adult Education at other campuses, including the University of Manitoba, the University of Alberta, the University of Victoria in British Colombia, the University of Guelph in Ontario, the University of Alaska, Northern Illinois University, and North Carolina State University, Raleigh.

I used a variety of teaching approaches for these courses. At the University of Manitoba, for example, I spent two days in the fall with the class in face-to-face meetings, then met with them via phone once a week for the fall term, and then once more met with them face to face at the end of the semester.

At North Carolina State University, Raleigh, I taught the class as a two-week summer school course for a delightful group of older students. Together we examined such fundamental questions as: What is the nature of human nature? How do we come to know something? What is of value in teaching? By the end of the course, we had explored the question of how do we as adults come to *know* something—and teaching strategies that can help adult learners reach this deeper level of learning. On the last day, my students asked me to join them at an open space outside the classroom where there were some picnic tables. Alcohol was not allowed in any North Carolina State University building (unlike on the UW–Madison campus, where beer was sold at the student union), but much to my surprise, in the center of one of the picnic tables were three huge bottles of wine. Each was labeled, one reading "What is human nature?"; one reading "How do we come to know?"; and one reading "What is of value?" They had clearly captured the essence of the course, and found a clever way of letting me know that, as we celebrated the end of the summer school session on a warm July day in Raleigh.

Using funds from McGraw-Hill and the vice chancellor's office at the UW–Madison, I continued my research projects, exploring how to improve the learning climate for older students returning to college campuses. I interviewed students and faculty at the University of Toronto; Temple University; the University of Michigan; North Carolina State University, Raleigh; and UW–Madison. I also interviewed adult education consultants Malcolm Knowles and Ralph Tyler. I published the results of this research in 1981 in *The Adult Learner on Campus: A Guide for Instructors and Administrators*.

Now that I had published several books on adult education, I began receiving frequent requests to speak at national higher education conferences across the country and in Canada.

February 13, 1981. Last Friday and Saturday I attended an adult education research conference at the University of Maryland. I gave the "wind-up" speech at the conference and was surprised to see more than 150 in attendance. Often on the last day of a conference people sneak out early.

I also began doing consulting work for organizations intent on expanding their continuing education opportunities.

April 22, 1981. I was in Minneapolis yesterday, working with the National Association of Music Educators. They have an increasing interest in adult education. It was a lively, interesting group with many ideas and lots of enthusiasm. They talked about such things as community bands, community singing, and adult music groups of various kinds. They put me up at the Hyatt Regency Hotel, which had only been open five weeks. I received the royal treatment. A live harp performance during breakfast was something new for me. So was a note from the manager welcoming me and matchbooks with my name on them. Room rate: $50.00 plus $5.00 tax.

In early March of 1982, Leo Walsh, dean of the College of Agricultural and Life Sciences, called me. I should have seen it coming. "Would you consider becoming chair of your department once more?" he asked. The dean said he knew I didn't want the job, but he had talked with several members of my department and they agreed to elect me if I agreed to serve. I said I would think about it.

March 16, 1982. I talked with Dean Walsh about becoming departmental chair. He said he would increase my salary to $52,000 and would offer whatever support he could if I would agree. He said he'd also talked with the other three deans to whom I would report, Dean Palmer in the School of Education, Dean McCubbin in the School of Family Resources and Consumer Sciences, and Dean VandeBerg in University of Wisconsin–Extension, and they agreed with Dean Walsh's suggestion that I become department chair once more.

Dean Walsh was my primary dean, and I met with him and with Dean VandeBerg several more times about once again having an appointment in Cooperative Extension. I had missed working with extension programs and looked forward to doing some work there in addition to my duties as department chair, plus research and departmental teaching. Was I crazy to accept so many divided responsibilities? Probably.

March 23, 1982. My new appointment as dept. chair: 51% extension, 15% research and 34% teaching.

April 8, 1982. Departmental election. Result: Apps for chair, Knox and Bjoraker for personnel committee.

14 Department Chair—Again

So now I was back doing administrative work as department chair. By 1982 the department had twelve secretaries in three locations. My administrative secretary, Mary Volkman, was also the immediate supervisor of the secretaries. We had about fifteen faculty members (also located in three buildings), eight or ten project and research assistants (graduate students working half-time), about a hundred graduate students (half working on master's degrees and half on PhDs), and about fifty undergraduates. On paper, the administrative structure—with the department chair reporting to three UW deans plus a UW–Extension dean and several faculty members with split appointments—looked impossible. It was nearly impossible in reality as well. I spent untold hours attending deans' meetings for department chairs.

I remember well the stories from those days—the serious, gut-wrenching ones, and, in equal number, the ones that proved hilarious. Soon after I became department chair, the university was recruiting departments to try the new Wang word processor computers. Up to this time, all of the secretarial staff worked on electric typewriters. I convinced Dean Walsh that because we

Badger Herald
July 22, 1982

CAVE ranks as best grad program

By JO ANN SMITH
Herald News Writer

The University of Wisconsin-Madison has a graduate school that has been ranked as the most respected graduate program in North America.

According to Jerold Apps, the department is called Continuing and Vocational Education or CAVE. Within that department, there is an adult education area. The national recognition was accredited to this area.

Apps, chairman of the department, said the program emphasizes teaching approaches for working with adults.

"We prepare students with master's and doctoral degrees in a variety of areas," Apps said. "A fair number of our graduate students are from Africa, the Far East and the Philippines. We have had a number of northern European students as well," he said.

According to Apps, many of these graduates work in hospitals and businesses, "Cuna Mutual and Oscar Mayer as well as other national firms are major providers for adult education," he said. "The graduates go back to work for the company in staff development, which is responsible for in-service training."

Apps also said one of the strengths of the graduate school is that each program is unique to each student. "We try to design each graduate student's program around the student's interests. No two programs are alike. We are willing to sit down

the international development program while many others work for international agricultural extensions.

"The students who attract from the United States are usually nurses, pharmacists, priests and nuns," Apps said. "It's not at all uncommon for a pastor to want a master's or doctorate degree in adult education because it is an important part of what churches are about these days," he added.

Apps also said many of the graduates work in ministries of education in

and fit a program into their backgrounds and their fields of interest," he said.

"Right now, we have 160 to 165 graduate students enrolled in the program with about 100 students who are not enrolled working on their dissertations or theses," he said.

"The average age of the graduate student in the adult education program is 38. They have usually worked five to 25 years before coming into the program," Apps said.

He said there were many reasons why the adult education program was rated number one in the country. "We are one of the largest adult education programs in this area," he said. "We are consciously trying to emphasize teaching, research and outreach," he added.

The reputations of the faculty, Apps said, as well as the reputation of the University of Wisconsin also contributed to the top ranking.

"We all do a fair amount of consulting, writing and research," Apps said. "Our publications are in

a variety of areas and they are used as textbooks and reference books in adult education throughout the country.

According to Apps, many of the professors work in the UW-Extension outreach program—in which the student can complete his degree at home rather than coming to the campus—as well as teach on campus and work on research.

Apps went on to explain why the reputation of the University of Wisconsin has contributed to the ranking. "We have very strong departments," he said. "Many of our students take classes in supporting departments such as sociology, psychology and computer sciences," he added.

"We have been a leader in continuing adult education since the turn of the century," Apps said. "We are expected to be good."

The survey which ranked the adult education program top in its area was conducted by *The Learning Connection*, a quarterly journal published by the Learning
(continued on page seven)

Regents approve UC refundable fee

By C.F. CLAUSEN
Assistant News Editor

The University of Wisconsin Board of Regents has reaffirmed United Council's mandatory refundable fee, despite requests from UW chancellors and

of the mandatory fee.

The mandatory fee process was initiated two years ago and requires that every student pay 50 cents per semester. If the student wants the money back, he or she must make a request in writing within 30 days of registering. The referendum on the

loss of as much as $100,000 in research funds.

genetically pure arose during an expanding the tests, they concluded that mice from Charles River, labeled "BALB/c," were a mixed population, not a pure strain.

The Charles River company is the world's largest producer of lab animals and has subsidiaries on three continents.

The white mice involved in the controversy are among the best studied and oldest of inbred strains, started in 1913 by Halsey Bagg, thus the name BALB for Bagg Albino.

The most important trait of the strain today is its tendency to develop cancer, especially myopia and lung cancer. It has become the standard animal in tumor biology

researchers re-evaluate their work.

Kahan explained that some experiments depend upon using inbred animals, which are nearly genetically identical. In inbred strains, no genetic difference exists between any two males or two females.

Kahan said the fact that the mice were not checked beforehand for impurities is comparable to going to the hospital to get saline solution. "You don't test to see if it's salty," she said.

It was therefore assumed that the mice were of the correct strain until problems arose. When the company
(continued on page seven)

In 1982, the Department of Continuing and Vocational Education was selected in a national survey as the top US graduate program offering degrees in adult and continuing education.

had twelve secretaries, we should receive at least two of the new word processors. He agreed, and they arrived in October.

October 21, 1982. Mary Volkman and I met with two women from the Wang Corporation to give us an overview on how to operate these new machines. We learned that to become proficient on a Wang Word Processor-Computer required about a week of training for the operator.

When I announced to the secretarial staff that we had these two new machines and that secretarial work would become much easier than pounding away on an IBM Selectric typewriter, I thought there would be a line of secretaries asking to use them. Soon a line of secretaries did indeed appear at my office door, but their reaction was the opposite from what I expected. Not one wanted to try the new word processor. In fact, more than one of the secretaries said that she would come in early and stay late as long as she didn't have to use one. Age didn't seem to matter; secretaries in their twenties were as opposed to these "newfangled" computers as those in their forties. I was dumfounded and turned to Mary Volkman, the oldest of the twelve.

"Mary, what are we going to do? I worked hard to get these new word processors, and the dean is going to ask me how they are working out," I said. "I can't tell him that every last secretary refused to use one."

Mary said quietly, "I'll enroll in the training session next week."

Soon the second word processor was out of the box and on a secretary's desk, and within a couple of months, nearly every secretary was asking when we would get additional machines. We had made the transition from typewriters to computers for the secretarial staff, but it didn't happen quickly. Ruth, who understood the challenges facing our staff, decided we should host some social activities for the secretaries and faculty in our department. This was especially important because our department was scattered across campus. The open houses were a lot of work for Ruth, and I applauded her for helping to make my job a bit easier. There was no question in my mind that the better people came to know each other, the better the working relationships would be.

December 22, 1982. On Saturday afternoon, Ruth and I invited the department's faculty, secretaries, and their spouses to our home for an open house celebra-

tion. Thirty-five people came. Ruth and I agree that it
is important for faculty, secretaries, and spouses to mix
together socially, and get to know each other outside of
their work environment.

During the second year of chairing the department,
I agreed to work with a visiting professor of adult education from Jordan. He wanted to observe my teaching and
research strategies and my administrative approach, as
well as become acquainted with other faculty members'
research and teaching. I had examined his background
quite carefully and was impressed with his accomplish-
ments, but I knew little of his personal life. A couple of
weeks before his arrival, I received a call from the US
State Department unit that awarded study visas.

"Are you Professor Apps?" the voice on the other
end asked.

"Yes," I answered. I had never received a call from
the State Department before and had no idea what this
person could want.

"I see that you have agreed to host a visiting professor from Jordan in your department."

"Yes," I answered again. I wondered if this chap from
Jordan had done something that would prevent him from
coming to the United States.

"Do you know that he has two wives?" the voice
asked.

"I did not know that," I answered.

"Will that be a problem in Madison, Wisconsin?"

"I don't think so," I said, chuckling.

The caller told me that the professor would arrive
that fall with only one of the wives; the second would join

them after the first of the year. "Just wanted to give you a heads-up," she said cheerily before ending the call.

The visiting professor was a joy to work with; we learned a good deal from him, and as the semester went on I hoped he was learning things from us as well. I had helped arrange for the visiting professor to rent an upstairs apartment from a faculty member in our department, George, who owned rental property near campus. Shortly after the first of the year, George stopped by to see me. He told my secretary that he had a critical problem to discuss. I wondered if one of his research proposals had been turned down—he had successfully gotten outside money for at least two proposals. But that was not the "critical problem" he had on his mind.

"Did you know our visiting professor from Jordan has two wives?" he asked.

"Yes, I knew that," I said. "But I understand he came with only one."

"Well, there are two wives living with him now; he introduced me to both of them!"

"I guess I should have told you the second wife was coming in January," I said.

"Well, now I've got a big problem," George said.

"Which is?"

"You know that two lesbians live in my first-floor apartment."

"Yes, I remember you telling me that," I replied.

"Our visiting professor from Jordan just learned about the details of his neighbors' relationship, and he's having a fit. He says he can't live in the same building with homosexuals."

I tried to hold back a smile.

"And you know what?" George continued. "The women in the first-floor apartment just learned about the visiting professor's two wives, and they said they can't live in the same building with a man with two wives. What are you going to do about it?"

Now I had to burst out laughing, for in what other place than Madison, Wisconsin, could such a conundrum rear its head?

"George," I said, "it's your rental property, and it's your problem. Good luck."

Of course, as department chair I often had to deal with matters of a much more serious nature. In 1983, one of our undergraduate students (I'll call him Jon here) was upset with his job opportunities after graduating from our department. I recorded the details of the case in my journal.

October 23, 1983. Jon, one of the department's undergraduate vocational agriculture majors came to me last spring complaining about the practice teaching grade that he'd gotten. He'd received a B. He was also not pleased with the less than positive letter of recommendation he had gotten from his supervising teacher at the practice teaching site. Now that he has graduated, he is requesting that he re-do his practice teaching. He is also asking that the university or Dr. [B.], his major professor, pay his tuition and the lost wages for a job that he never got. So, we had a meeting in my office. Dr. B., M. W., who directs the practice teaching program, H. L., the assistant dean in the School of Education, B. M. from the chancellor's office, G. K. from the UW's attorney's office, and me. We met a half hour with the student and then another hour and a half without him. I was asked to get further information about his practice teaching in a high school near Madison. I'm to find out whether or not his practice teaching experience met the minimum requirements. [I did this and learned that his teaching had been considered mediocre.] There is a possibility that the student will file a lawsuit against our department and the university. His argument: a poor grade and a less than stellar letter of recommendation from his supervising teacher led to his not being hired as a vocational agriculture instructor.

These sorts of problem take so much time and so much emotional energy.

November 7, 1983. Jon, the student with the grievance, stopped by this afternoon. He ranted on for more than an hour. He asked for a copy of the evaluation from his supervising teacher, which I gave him. He read it and then threw the paper into the air saying the supervising teacher had not told the truth about the experience he'd had. Several times he yelled, "My diploma from the university isn't worth the paper it's written on."

I suggested to him that there were other jobs in agriculture beyond teaching vocational agriculture and that he should stop by the College of Agriculture's Job Placement office.

I wonder when all of this will end?

November 26, 1983. The group reviewing Jon's case for a grade change met once more and agreed to deny his request.

Jon hired an attorney, who met with me in my office to inform me that he was considering filing a lawsuit against Professor B., me, and our department. I explained to the attorney the details of the case from the department's perspective, adding that the university does not guarantee jobs for its graduates, although, I said, "Those who do well, especially in Jon's field, are almost always hired."

I went on to explain that high schools seeking to employ new teachers put considerable weight not only on the student's grades in regular classes but also on his or her performance as a practice teacher. Here is where Jon did not do so well, I explained.

After an hour-long discussion, Jon's attorney said, "I don't think he has a case." I did not hear from Jon again.

That was just one of several problems I faced as department chair of a midsize university department. The following year, 1984, proved even more challenging.

March 29, 1984. I leave for Eau Claire this afternoon where I will give a speech at a returning student conference. High stress time. My PhD students are turning in dissertations for reading. Merit increase money must be allocated to faculty. The department received 3.5% of its total base salary of staff for raises. It is the responsibility of the personnel committee, which I chair, to decide who gets a raise and who doesn't, and how much the raise will be. I had it all figured out, and then UW–Extension pulled back its merit increase for three of our faculty with extension appointments, so I must do it all over again.

April 18, 1984. The frustration continues. I feel like a pebble in a fast moving stream, bouncing here and here, but having little control over what I do.

June 26, 1984. This past spring I had one tension-loaded experience after another: negotiating office space for several faculty (a couple were not pleased with the result), hiring a new person for business education, and giving several keynote speeches. I had planned to spend some time working on another continuing education book—but had to put off the writing.

Thankfully, I had my farm in central Wisconsin as a place to retreat from the challenges of administration. Though the kids were mostly grown (Sue was about to start her first elementary teaching job, Steve was a junior at Winona State University, and Jeff was a sophomore at UW–Madison), they would be around more in the summer, and I looked forward to spending time with them and working in our big garden. On a spring day at the farm, I wrote:

May 6, 1984. Beautiful Sunday morning. Clear blue sky. Birds singing—catbirds, robins, wrens. Bluebirds in the birdhouse by the cabin. Peaceful. No phone ringing. Nobody knocking at the cabin door.

But the challenges continued through the summer and into the fall.

August 2, 1984. We interviewed two candidates for an open position we have in vocational agriculture. Today we are interviewing one more. I certainly hope this third person has more ability than the first two we've seen. I doubt either of them could do the research necessary to earn tenure.

August 7, 1984. We interviewed a third person for the open position. He had promise, but was prone to use sexist language when he talked. Professor G., a woman on our staff, took issue with his behavior and spoke against him at the personnel committee meeting, of which she is a part. Yesterday she wrote a blistering memo to the entire department faculty where she pointed out in great detail this young man's "sexist transgressions." I don't defend what he did, but Professor G. stepped beyond the boundaries of decency, and perhaps even the law, with what she did. I met with her and suggested that her letter, which the young man also saw, could later be used in a lawsuit if we hired him and at some later date if he was denied tenure. He would have evidence that at least one faculty member was against him from the very beginning. Professor G.'s only comment was that she wasn't aware of this potential problem when she wrote the memo. So go the challenges of being a department chair.

Low-enrollment courses at the university had become an issue in 1984. Cost effectiveness—meaning how many students taught per instructor—was the mantra of some of our top-level administrators. If enrollment fell below a certain number, the department had to provide an explanation for continuing the class.

October 3, 1984. I received a memo from an associate dean. She has done it again. She said my reasons for keeping low-enrollment courses in the department were not sufficient and I must rewrite the report. The implication was that low-enrollment courses should be dropped—*when the semester is half over*? I will not drop

any course this late in the semester. This associate dean
is one of those rule-bound persons with both eyes riv-
eted on the rulebook but with no vision for the future—
or for exceptions to the rules.

I looked forward to completing my five-year term—
and second stint—as department chair, and to celebrating our first ten years as a newly reorganized department. Some naysayers had said we wouldn't last a year.
We had made it to a decade.

January 18, 1985. Today we are celebrating our department's 10 years of existence with a program this afternoon and a banquet this evening.

In 1985 I was fifty-one years old, tired, and wanting
to go back to full-time teaching and research without the
additional challenges of administration. I thought about
friends who worked for Cooperative Extension who had
retired at age fifty-five.

September 19, 1985. I could retire when I reach age 55,
which will be July 25, 1989. Should I turn to full-time
writing, something I've long wanted to do, or continue
teaching for several more years? My retirement benefits will be much greater if I hold off on retirement
until I am at least 60.

But thoughts of early retirement would have to remain in the background. There were meetings to attend,
personnel problems to solve, budgets to develop, and a
bevy of deans and associate deans to contend with.

October 22, 1985. Meetings from 10:00 a.m. to 2:00 p.m. Mostly on staffing and staffing plans. Much talk—slow, tedious.

February 3, 1986. The Gramm-Rudman Federal Bill to balance the federal budget coupled with cuts in state spending make for difficult times. Today I will meet with Dean Walsh from CALS and Dean Koval of Cooperative Extension to learn how the budget cuts may affect our faculty budgeted in CALS.

February 14, 1986. We have a department faculty meeting this morning. With serious budget cuts, the department will be losing several positions within the next year or so, and this has the faculty upset. Mary, our department's administrative secretary, is retiring, so we must make plans for that position.

March 10, 1986. I spent almost all of Saturday and a couple hours on Sunday at the office, reading faculty annual reports. Today the department personnel committee will meet to decide the relative ranking (according to productivity) of our faculty. I'm also spending much time on budget matters. With federal and state cutbacks, I must shave up to $40,000 from our CALS budget alone. One alternative is to move people from 12-month appointments to 9 months. I am seriously considering this for myself, to set an example.

March 11, 1986. It is time to do the annual performance evaluation of each faculty member in the department. The Personnel Committee, consisting of Sara Steele, Jim Stone, John Thompson, Wendy Way, and me as chair, are to place each faculty person in one of four groups: high, high middle, low middle, and low. It's a long, grueling process.

March 28, 1986. Budget work all week. I've been figuring salaries for faculty. Next Wednesday I meet with the deans in agriculture to discuss the increases and inform them which faculty will move from 12-month to 9-month appointments. I am one of those who will switch.

April 12, 1986. Ten a.m. department meeting that went on and on, and on and finally ended at 12:45. Big argument about graduate student admission procedures. We discussed a fundamental issue: what are appropriate admission standards to maintain quality in our graduate program and yet not discourage students from applying, especially international students?

June 30, 1986. Today is my last day on a federal appointment with Cooperative Extension. Tomorrow my appointment goes to 50% teaching, 40% research, and 19% Extension. And I go to a nine-month appointment with extra pay if I teach during summer school.

In June Mary Volkman announced her retirement as administrative secretary. Her absence left a huge hole in the department. Mary had supervised our secretarial work with a gentle hand. She got along well with all of the secretaries, and at the same time she had the respect of the faculty. She was an excellent administrator who knew how to deal with details, organize her time, and still approach each day with a smile on her face.

After she left, one of the deans called me and said he had the perfect person to fill Mary's position. I relied on the dean's judgment, and I hired her. (I'll call her Jody here.)

August 26, 1986. We have hired a new administrative secretary, one recommended to us by one of the deans. Jody is having difficulty adjusting to her new position as administrative secretary and is especially having difficulty adjusting to Professor G., who is a full professor in the department and has written several blistering memos to Jody, about her work. Most of the complaints I would say are petty things. Dealing with this takes so much energy.

September 10, 1986. Jody is slowly learning her duties. I believe the job is much more complicated than she thought it would be.

Meanwhile, I was looking forward to wrapping up my tenure as department chair.

November 4, 1986. I talked with Dean Walsh last Friday and he is not opposed to my stepping down from the departmental chair position next year. He had hoped I would do it indefinitely, however. I said I would support Robert Ray for the position—Bob has been working with me as Assistant Dept. Chair. The Dean also asked if I would be interested in the Associate Dean for Social Sciences position in the College. I told him I really wanted to go back to teaching, researching, and writing.

With a change in the governor's office in November of 1986, challenges at the university took on a new level of concern.

November 5, 1986. Governor Anthony Earl, seeking a second term, was beaten by Republican Tommy Thompson. Thompson vows to cut state spending and boost business. He says we can't afford a "world class" university and must take another 5 percent budget cut. Tough times ahead for the university, I fear.

And within the department, Jody continued to be challenged at every turn.

November 17, 1986. Jody continues to have problems with secretaries in the department whom she supervises. One, a woman in her 60s, fell a few weeks ago and has her arm in a sling. Tough to type with one arm in a sling. Then last week, on a morning when we had a half-inch of snow, she fell again. And, yes, she sprained the other wrist so she couldn't type at all. What does a secretary with two incapacitated arms do? Jody passed the question on to me last week.

In 1986, the College of Agricultural and Life Sciences was in the midst of developing a comprehensive long-range plan. It was while I was serving on one of the planning committees that I got a surprise call from Dean Walsh. He told me I would be able to leave my department chair assignment a few months early if I agreed to help him with an assignment.

December 27, 1986. CALS Dean Walsh asked if I'd write the final report for the long-range planning committee for the college. I said I couldn't do it and chair the department at the same time. He said, "You're leaving the chair position in summer anyway, why don't you leave a few months early?" So on December 22, I sent a letter to the faculty and staff in my department saying that I am stepping down as chair on February 1, 1987. I also sent along a nomination form so a new chair can be nominated for an election to be held on January 23. Several faculty members were surprised when they learned of my plans.

Reflecting on my years as department chair, nearly seven in total, I remember the good and the bad, and I especially remember what I learned from the experience.

I learned the value of patience. My father had drummed this into me starting when I was a little kid, but now I had learned in spades how to be patient. Faculty governance, where the faculty decide on everything from what is taught to who is hired to teach, is important. But it takes time. Lots of time.

I learned how to deal with difficult people. One of the associate deans took the prize for being the most rule-bound, noncreative person I ever worked with.

And I learned to deal with incompetence. In a February 1987 journal entry, I wrote:

Jody's bright, but she's the most disorganized person I've ever met. Her desk has papers piled everywhere, important papers, personnel action forms, budget sheets, phone messages, with the heap growing ever taller. One time when I was away to a conference, she took all of the mail, unopened, and tossed it under her desk. "No sense opening it when you're not here," she said, never thinking that she might need to contact me about some of the correspondence, or that she might reply to some of it herself.

I also learned that some problems can be easily solved—and that I didn't have to be involved in solving them. When I accepted the chair position, I negotiated with the department that I would not be in my office until 9:00 a.m. each day. I argued that I wanted the time slot from seven to nine each morning for my own research and writing. As it turned out, many of the little problems that would develop on a typical day would either have gone away or had been solved by the time I arrived at nine.

I discovered an effective leadership style—one that I learned about in my research and that mostly worked in practice. The essence of it is this: hire good people and stay out of their way—they will amaze you with what they accomplish. To use a farm metaphor, sometimes it's necessary to clear the brush out of the way. I did my share of brush-clearing while chairing the department, meaning I made sure staff had good secretarial help, had good office spaces, and weren't hassled by associate deans, among other duties.

I also learned that occasionally—just as I remembered from my days managing a cucumber salting station in little Wild Rose, Wisconsin, in the early 1950s—some employees needed hand-holding and encouragement, and others needed a kick in the pants to get them back on track.

I took those lessons with me as I settled into my position as past chair, once again a regular professor.

February 2, 1987. Today is my first day at the office as an ordinary professor since 1982, when I became chair for the second time. I've now been chair for six and one-half years, which is half the time our department has existed. Last Thursday I moved offices—I exchanged with Bob Ray, who is the new chair. Room 276, Teacher Education Building, is where I now hold forth. I have two major projects this spring: the new Jossey-Bass book I'm working on, and the long-range plan I am writing for CALS. I'll split my time between the two projects. It will take me a few weeks, I'm afraid, to shift gears from the near frantic pace associated with the chair position. I'm not accustomed to working on any project for more than a few minutes without a phone call or some other interruption.

April 6, 1987. Thursday I received a letter from the chair of the search committee for a new dean of Cooperative Extension saying I was nominated for the position. I refrained from writing on the bottom of letter "You've got to be kidding" and returning it. But I didn't—not yet, anyway.

15 Leadership Development

Leaving the work of department chair behind did not mean I no longer had to concern myself with bureaucratic matters. With declining state support for public universities, especially for the large research universities, the pressure was on all faculty to find outside funding sources that would support our research. These sources included federal government programs and large foundations. The financial support I received from the College of Agricultural and Life Sciences Research Division was usually enough to support just a half-time research assistant, so I worked hard to identify and pursue other funding sources.

CALS had a long relationship with the Kellogg Foundation, going back to the mid-1950s when the foundation supported a program to help agricultural extension administrators from across the country complete master's and PhD degrees through what was then called the Department of Agricultural and Extension Education. The relationship had lapsed, however, after the reorganization of the UW's extension programs.

Several of us in the Department of Continuing and Vocational Education worked on reestablishing the con-

nection, and by 1986 the Kellogg Foundation had agreed
to fund a program for newly hired professors of adult education from the United States and Canada, designed to
assist them with everything from research strategies and
publication tips to approaches for achieving tenure. The
program was based in CAVE with Alan Knox, Jack Ferver,
and me in charge. We hired Judy Adrian, one of my PhD
students, as a half-time project assistant.

In October of 1987, Knox, Ferver, and I met with
Arlon Elser from the Kellogg Foundation to discuss the
possibility of another grant to continue the new adult
education professor program in 1988. A few months
later, the foundation approved a grant of eighty-five
thousand dollars to continue the program.

On November 3, 1988, I met with Elser in Tulsa,
Oklahoma, at his request, to discuss other proposals that
I might submit to the foundation for funding. It was the
beginning of a long journey of meetings, phone conversations, brainstorming, and draft proposal writing. It
felt like a kind of dance, in which I was trying to figure
out the music the foundation was playing and what dance
steps I should use. I drafted a proposal, trying to follow Elser's suggestions while keeping our department's
needs at the fore.

> September 5, 1989, Sarasota, Florida. Alan Knox and I
> spent two hours with Arlon Elser talking about the draft
> proposal I had submitted to him. Sometimes I wonder
> why I go chasing this kind of money. It can be so very
> frustrating. Elser asked several questions about the
> proposal. Some of his points were well made. I'll have
> to do some revising when I return to Madison. My pes-
> simistic thought is: we have a very limited chance of

landing the money. Elser, in passing, mentioned that
Kellogg turns down 99% of the proposals they receive.

Meanwhile, on March 7, 1989, extension chancellor
Pat Boyle had asked me to attend a meeting in Eau Claire
with Pat Borich, director of Cooperative Extension for
Minnesota. The purpose of the meeting was to develop
a different proposal for the Kellogg Foundation. At this
meeting we discussed an idea for a training program for
Cooperative Extension administrators. Many longtime
administrators would soon be retiring, and the program
would help prepare those who would be seeking these
positions in a few years. Another grant proposal to the
Kellogg Foundation was soon in the works.

In June 1989, we received the bad news: Kellogg
had turned down our first grant proposal. I had already
begun working on several projects outlined in the proposal. Now that work was all in the trash can. The music
had stopped. The dance was over.

While I was doing the fund-raising dance, I continued
my outreach efforts around the country. I served as an
external examiner for PhD students completing their
work at the University of Toronto, and I worked as a
consultant to the New York State Board of Higher Education, evaluating doctoral programs in higher education at Syracuse, Cornell, and Columbia Universities. I
had a similar assignment with Ontario's Board of Higher
Education, where I served as an evaluator for continuing and higher education programs at the University of
Guelph. I also served on panels—usually with one or two
others—to evaluate continuing and higher education
graduate programs at Mississippi State University; North

Carolina State University, Raleigh; and the University of Minnesota.

I occasionally worked with continuing and higher education departments that needed outside assistance with strategic planning. At the University of Alberta, Edmonton, the assignment proved more challenging than I had anticipated.

Department chair Abe Konrad had arranged for all the members of his department to meet at a resort hotel in Banff, Alberta—one of the most beautiful places in North America. The department members arrived at noon on a Monday and spent the afternoon in workshop sessions discussing their department's research, graduate program, and resource needs. I thought the group of twelve faculty members was off to a bad start when they began raising questions about the intent of the retreat instead of focusing on planning for the future. But that changed over the course of the day.

May 10, 1988. Once the faculty moved into small groups, they came up with some useful ideas and perspectives. For instance, the research group said a long-range goal for the department was to change the attitude in the department that teaching is more important than research—the current situation—to an attitude that research and teaching should be of equal importance. They say it, and seem to agree, but I'm not so sure they believe it. I think maybe a third of the faculty believe this should happen. I'm curious how the discussions will go tomorrow.

May 11, 1988. A long day of wrangling about departmental intention and how to get there. I think we've made progress, but it's slow and difficult. Two or three of the department's faculty seem intent on "doing in" the department's new direction and Abe Konrad's leadership.

This interaction was fairly typical of my experience with higher education consulting. At one point during the discussions, faculty members with differing opinions began shouting at one another. I suggested that the entire group take a break, go outside, and enjoy the mountain scenery for a half hour. When they returned to the meeting room, they continued to debate, but in a considerably more civil manner.

Invitations to speak at adult and continuing education conferences arrived frequently in the late 1980s, taking me to events from Washington, DC, to Tucson to Tallahassee. In December 1988, I gave the keynote speech—on the topic "What do adult learners want?"— for an audience of four hundred at the national meeting of the Learning Resources Network.

Our department collaborated with the Learning Resources Network, based in Manhattan, Kansas, to sponsor an annual summer workshop in Madison for practitioners and administrators in adult and continuing education from across North America.

July 9, 1987. Today marks the third day of the third Madison Institute for Adult Learning. Twenty people are enrolled. They come from Wisconsin, Texas, New Jersey, Iowa, Michigan, Ohio, Indiana—12 states represented. They came from UW–Stout, UW–Platteville, La Crosse Voc. Tech, community college programs, hospital programs and continuing and higher education programs. They shared ideas, wrestled with new ones presented by

The College Board
Presents a National Conference on

LIFELONG EDUCATION IN AMERICA: BECOMING A "NATION OF STUDENTS"

November 18-19, 1991 • Washington, D.C.

- What role should colleges and universities play in providing learning opportunities to individuals over a lifetime?
- How can colleges and universities be more responsive to the lifelong education imperatives of the population?
- How will this trend impact your institution?

Find out by attending the College Board's national conference on Lifelong Education.

Featuring:

Jerold Apps, University of Wisconsin

I spoke at the National Conference on Lifelong Education in America, Washington, DC, in 1991.

our staff, and found the institute of considerable value, according to the evaluation forms submitted.

• • •

By summer 1990, a new dance had started up with the Kellogg Foundation, with a different orchestra and new tunes. The prospects for the proposal that Pat Boyle, Pat Borich, and I had worked on together began to look promising.

July 2, 1990. I met with Chancellor Boyle on Friday to discuss the latest Kellogg proposal, which is titled "A Proposal for a National Center for Extension Leadership Development (NELD)." Pat asked me if I would direct the project if it was funded. It would be a half-time assignment with the other half of my time devoted to my regular professorial duties. We discussed some of

the potential responsibilities for the director position.
I said I would have to discuss this with Ruth before giving him a decision.

I was up for the new challenge, and Ruth agreed
that I should do it. I let Pat know that I was in. Based
on my recent experience with Kellogg, my hopes were
not high that the proposal would receive funding. This
time, several national university leaders, including the
national Extension Committee on Policy (ECOP), had
been involved in fine-tuning the proposal and were
working to convince Kellogg to fund it. When ECOP
learned that Kellogg was considering funding the
program, they asked other states to apply for the NELD
center where the program would be located. Of course,
Wisconsin applied.

In late July 1990, the ECOP selection team visited
Wisconsin, and on August 15 we received word that University of Wisconsin–Extension had been selected for
the national leadership development program. As the
program's director, I would work half-time on the project during the regular school year and full-time during
the summer. With the funding approval, it was full speed
ahead to organize the program, establish an office, hire
staff, create application forms and selection criteria for
interns, and attend to a hundred more details.

Kellogg would provide starter money to help
establish the new program. After three years, the
program would have to be funded without Kellogg's
monetary assistance. In addition, the foundation grant
required partnership funding: Kellogg would provide
$2,073,300 for three years and the state Cooperative
Extension programs would provide $3,768,700, making

the three-year total budget for the program $5,842,000. However, I had access to only the $2 million–plus for the various program activities and support money, including travel expenses, for the interns. We planned to enlist three groups of interns, ten in 1991, thirty in 1992, and thirty in 1993. In addition to the intern program, the NELD proposal called for two workshops for current extension deans and directors and a national meeting for land-grant university presidents with a focus on new directions for adult and continuing education programs.

With a new office in the Madison campus extension building, I was back to having two offices. I bought surplus furniture, desks, file cabinets, and chairs, hired a program director (my PhD student Judy Adrian), found a part-time secretary, selected a national curriculum advisory committee to help develop the content for the program, and began figuring out how to manage the budget. The Kellogg Foundation money would come to the UW–Extension Business Office, whom I would work with on all matters related to the disbursement of funds. The business office had its rules—and they enforced them to the letter. Unfortunately, several of the activities that we had planned for the NELD interns and for which we needed the release of Kellogg funds appeared outside their guidelines for "legitimate" disbursement. I attempted to negotiate with them (not always successfully) as I did not want to compromise what I considered an important approach to conducting leadership development—much of it experiential, meaning the interns experienced the curriculum directly rather than merely reading about leadership theory in books.

On January 8, 1991, the newly formed NELD Curriculum Committee arrived in Madison, and we met for two days working on program details. Judy Adrian and I had spent many hours prior to the advisory committee meeting working out program details. With a few tweaks here and there, the committee gave us the thumbs-up to proceed.

The curriculum included three phases: diversity training, an international experience, and development of an individual philosophy of leadership for each participant.

On February 13, 1991, I met with Dan Moore, my contact person with the Kellogg Foundation, to discuss our progress and plans. Dan suggested we immediately enlist someone to do an ongoing evaluation of the program, and I suggested Professor Boyd Rossing, one of my colleagues in the Department of Continuing and Vocational Education. Boyd accepted the invitation to become a part of our team.

Next I met with ECOP at their regular meeting in San Antonio, Texas, to update them on our plans. And for several days in March, the NELD national advisory committee met in Madison to help us think through the detailed directions for the program. The advisory committee included a representative from Kellogg, three businesspeople, two university vice presidents, and several extension directors and associate directors. One member took issue with our plans, while the rest were very supportive. I listened carefully to what the critic had to say, but in the end I went along with the directions provided by the committee's majority.

In June 1991, our first group of NELD interns, ten of them, arrived in Madison.

June 11, 1991. This morning, routine work. Introduc-
tions, overview of program. After lunch we walked to
the Memorial Union on campus, climbed into canoes
and paddled a considerable distance to Willow Beach
under the direction of Chris Henricks, a former Out-
ward Bound leader. Several had never been in a canoe.
Two in a canoe. Who leads and who follows?

One of my goals for the program—a goal that often
got me in trouble with the business office—was to have
the interns experience leadership with hands-on activities. Following the activity, we discussed the experience, including what they believed they had learned
and how they might apply it to leadership situations. I
asked the interns to keep a journal of everything they
experienced as they moved through the year-long set
of activities. A few of them grumbled about writing in a
journal, but they all did it. They quickly came to understand that I am a firm believer in the power of writing as
an aid to learning, especially when it comes to thinking
through the meaning of something—for example, what
does two people paddling a canoe have to do with leadership development?

We conducted several weeklong workshops in each
of the three years for each of the three intern groups.
One year we took a trip to Europe, where we studied the
early efforts toward developing the European Union.
Another time we traveled to Mexico and studied the debate over the development of the North American Free
Trade Agreement. In one of our most enlightening ad-
ventures, we stayed on the Mandan Indian reservation
in North Dakota and canoe-camped from the Garrison
Dam on the Missouri River on our way to Bismarck. A

Mandan shaman helped the interns better understand and interpret what they had experienced while living on the reservation. Each evening, he shared the Mandan creation story and the significance of cultural activities, including the sweat lodge, which several interns later experienced. Through storytelling, he helped the interns experience the power of story as a way of communicating facts, multiple perspectives, and emotion.

A few months later, we spent a week on the Mescalero-Apache reservation in New Mexico, experiencing a personal relationship with this tribe and learning about their culture, history, economic challenges, and much more.

For two weeks during the summer of 1992, we studied the history of the civil rights movement, working out of Tuskegee University in Alabama and living with African American families in that state. We visited Montgomery and the church where Martin Luther King Jr. spoke. We

NELD interns set off to canoe the Missouri River from the Garrison Dam to Bismarck, North Dakota, in 1992.

Paige Baker, a Mandan/Hidatsa tribal member, introduced our NELD interns to the sweat lodge tradition.

Mandan/Hidatsa children performed a ceremonial dance for NELD interns and staff.

walked across the notorious Edmund Pettus Bridge in Selma. We studied the research of George Washington Carver and Booker T. Washington, early Tuskegee leaders. For those two weeks, I hired an African American community development specialist who had been active in the civil rights movement in the 1960s. He had been involved in many protests and been jailed several times for his activities, and he had many interesting first-person stories to share with our group.

> May 1, 1992. Tuskegee Inn, Tuskegee, Alabama. Meeting of Interns to discuss what they experienced during the week, and what they had learned. We broke into small groups. Directions to the groups: What happened during the week? What were your emotions and frustrations?
>
> Summary points: As a leader, allow yourself to be human at all times. Work with courage and compassion, especially with compassion for those who are different from you. Need for integrity in one's personal life, work life, and community life. People we visited have warmth, courage, and candor. We marveled at those whose lives have been filled with personal tragedy yet continue to have faith in the future. People we visited were rich in human spirit and poor in material possessions.

The NELD national conference designed for state university presidents proved the most challenging of everything we attempted. Some 250 university presidents and top-level university administrators attended the conference in La Jolla, California, in February of 1993. I worked with a national planning committee for several months to plan the event, which was to focus on future directions for state university outreach programs. I was confident that all was in order. But then, on the day before the conference opened, the keynote speaker called to say his wife was seriously ill and he could not come. Panic. I called together my staff and the members of the planning committee for a long Sunday afternoon meeting to decide what to do. They decided I should give the keynote speech. So without any reference materials, I spent Sunday evening writing a speech, which I gave the following morning, with knees knocking and a dry mouth. I was told it went over well. The rest of the conference was a breeze.

Looking back now, I see the National Center for Extension Leadership Development program as the capstone of the thirty-eight years I worked for UW–Madison and UW–Extension. It was the most challenging and the most satisfying educational program I was ever involved with. I dearly loved teaching on the Madison campus, and my graduate students were outstanding in every way. But with NELD, I didn't have to worry about keeping track of the hours I was teaching, I gave no grades, and there were no examinations. Most of the teaching was nontraditional: hands-on learning outside of a typical classroom, in settings across the United States and around the world.

From a research perspective, the NELD program gave me an opportunity to test firsthand a model I had developed for developing a personal philosophy of leadership, an adaptation of a model I had earlier developed for teachers working in adult and continuing education. As we worked through the three years of the program, I tweaked and fine-tuned the model, and that research appeared in my 1994 book *Leadership for the Emerging Age: Transforming Practice in Adult and Continuing Education*.

Time was always a challenge with the NELD program. Even with three years to conduct the program, it seemed we never had enough time to plan our events. That might actually have been a good thing, as some of my academic friends and I occasionally "overplanned" and spent untold hours in planning meetings. With NELD, it was plan and then produce, learn from the event, and plan the next one. It helped to have a tireless team of excellent staff: program director Judy Adrian, secretary Melissa Meyer, program assistant Tim Neuman, and Dr. Boyd Rossing, who evaluated all activities.

Judy Adrian and Boyd Rossing

Members of our national advisory committee challenged us, as was their role. Were our ideas too "out there," and were the participants ready for what we were doing? This was a fair criticism, and I listened to it. I worked hard to start where the participants were and then worked just as hard to move them beyond where they were.

The most difficult criticism we received came from the UW–Extension Business Office, through which all of the Kellogg money for the program flowed. I have no doubt part of the problem was my fault, in not taking enough time to explain that what we were doing wasn't a typical classroom program. For example, when we lived on the Mandan Indian Reservation in North Dakota, we decided the participants would learn more of the Mandan culture if we had a buffalo roast, complete with traditional dancing. So I bought a buffalo in Bismarck and had it prepared. When I submitted the invoice to the business office, the staff informed me that they could not approve the purchase of a buffalo. On the returned invoice I crossed off "buffalo" and wrote in "meat." The invoice was approved.

The positive features of the NELD program many times outweighed the often petty roadblocks that we faced in conducting the program. Not only did I learn much about new approaches to hands-on teaching, but I learned how to work my way through a bureaucracy that often stood in the way of anything "new."

I wrote a message and included it in my final speech to our program interns. Today I believe it speaks to all who live in this world and don't make time to experience it, and to those who fail to see the power of positive relationships with our fellow human beings.

No matter where your journey will take you,
May you always have mountains to climb
And the strength to climb them.
Wildflowers to see
And the patience to see them.
New paths to follow
And the courage to walk them.
May you have each other
For support and joy,
For encouragement and love.
And may you always have each other to listen
When no one else will hear.

Forty-five years is a long time to be associated with one institution. I am forever grateful to so many for the opportunity. *Courtesy of the UW–Madison Archives, #S10273*

Epilogue

Starting with the autumn day in 1951 when I walked on to the University of Wisconsin–Madison campus as a new freshman, I was associated with the UW in one way or another for nearly forty-five years. I could have stayed longer (and many of my colleagues said I should have), but I officially retired on January 8, 1994, at age fifty-nine.

For many years I had wanted to work full-time as a writer. Robert Gard, my writing mentor, had given me the excellent advice to keep my day job, teaching at the UW, until our children were through college and our expenses less. But now I was ready.

Still, it was not an easy decision to leave the university. I loved the place. Starting in late fall 1992, Ruth and I had long discussions about my retirement plans. When I met with the chair of our department and told him my plans, he asked, "Why are you retiring so early? You're at the peak of your career." I told him I wanted to research and write, do some consulting, and do a little teaching.

He shook his head. "That's what you are doing now," he said.

I could see the truth in his statement. But I had just completed four years of half-time work with the NELD leadership development project. I was tired. I wanted to steer away from committees and administrative work. I wanted to focus on ideas and writing and do more digging into rural history, especially the history of Upper Midwest farms and small towns.

To make the transition from the university easier, and to continue working with my graduate students who had not completed their degrees, I agreed to work 30 percent of full-time during the 1994 and 1995 school years. I taught my Philosophy of Adult Education course each semester for those years and helped my graduate students complete their degrees. I spent two days a week at my office, where I would meet with students. In the fall of 1995, my responsibilities at the University of Wisconsin–Madison and the University of Wisconsin–Extension ended.

Now, more than twenty years later, I can look back with a mostly clear eye and reflect on what I learned from the experience.

I was the first one in my family to attend college. In my wildest imagination, I had never thought that one day I would become a college professor. I came from a family of farmers, and most of the young people of my father and mother's generation had not graduated from elementary school. When they were big enough to work, they went to work on the farm. The tuition scholarship I received when I graduated from high school, my father's permission to attend college, and my mother's unending support made all the difference.

Throughout college and my career, I constantly fought an internal battle. From the time I had polio at age twelve, my confidence had been at rock bottom. And as I started my university career, a small voice told me, "Fella, you are in way over your head. Besides, where'd you ever get the idea that you could be a college professor?" It had not been my idea. I was quite happy as a county extension agent, working with farmers and dealing with topics that I knew and loved. It was other people who encouraged me to do things that I didn't think I was capable of doing. All along the way, many people—Professor Walter Bjoraker, Professor (later Chancellor) Patrick Boyle, Professor Robert Gard, and of course my wife, Ruth, and many others—were there to encourage and support me.

And I discovered I could do it. Not only could I teach college students, but I loved doing it. As my college teaching years flew by, I gained confidence—even though that dark specter from my polio days never quite went away.

Teaching and doing research at a major university gave me the opportunity to explore ideas, to take them apart and examine them, and to try them out in my writing, in my off-campus outreach work, and in my on-campus teaching. A graduate course in educational philosophy that I took in 1965 gave me the idea for what became a career-long exploration of what I called "developing a personal philosophy of adult education." The essence of the idea was for those in teaching roles to explore their basic beliefs about students, about the content taught, and about the teaching methods used. I argued that by examining and developing a practical personal philosophy of education, teachers would have a solid foundation for their work, would be better teachers, and would enjoy what they were doing.

I am a firm believer in lifelong learning. For every book I write, whether it is fiction or nonfiction, I spend many hours researching and learning as much as I can about my subject. I will also forever be a teacher. One of the reasons I write is to share the results of what I learn both through research and through experience.

Since leaving the University of Wisconsin, I have continued teaching workshops for adults. In 1995 and 1997, I taught leadership workshops for the University of Alaska on Yukon Island. Students lived in tents on the beach, and Ruth and I stayed in a little cabin with no plumbing or electricity. Twenty-plus graduate students from all over Alaska attended. I continue to teach creative writing workshops (currently in my twenty-eighth year) at The Clearing in Door County, Wisconsin, as well as at several community libraries.

In the past decade, I've slowly become aware of an anti-intellectual movement happening in many places in the country, including Wisconsin. People complain

Students arrive by boat for a summer workshop I taught in 1997 on Yukon Island, Alaska.

that "ordinary folks"—which in this mindset means those without college degrees or postsecondary education of any kind—are somehow better fitted for public office and have a better understanding of how tax dollars should be spent and environmental concerns debated than those who have college education. University researchers who create research questions and share results that are counter to local beliefs are poo-pooed and discounted as irrelevant, impractical, or an impediment to financial gains. And even professors themselves have come under fire, criticized at best as overpaid and at worst as lazy elitists.

I suspect some of the blame for the emergence of this anti-intellectual attitude can be placed at the feet of the university, which clearly has not done enough to help citizens understand the university's purpose and its contributions through its teaching, research, and outreach programs.

I wholeheartedly believe that local people, no matter what their level of education, should have an active voice in local decisions. But to deny relevant information that will make for better, more informed decisions seems shortsighted—and even dangerous in some situations, especially when the decisions involve human health and long-range environmental impacts.

These days I'm happy to be writing full-time, teaching short courses in writing, lecturing about rural history, and doing radio and television work on these topics. But seldom a day goes by that I do not think of those wonderful years I spent on the Madison campus of the University of Wisconsin. It was a great privilege to be there.

Notes

CHAPTER 5
1. "The Vietnam War: The Jungle War, 1965–1968," The History Place, www.historyplace.com/unitedstates/vietnam/index-1965.html.
2. "1960–1969," UW Archives and Records Management, University of Wisconsin–Madison Libraries, www.library.wisc.edu/archives/exhibits/campus-history-projects/protests-social-action-at-uw-madison-during-the-20th-century/1960-1969.

CHAPTER 6
1. "Enrollments 1888 to Present," Office of the Registrar, University of Wisconsin–Madison, https://registrar.wisc.edu/enrollments_1888_to_present.htm.
2. Matthew Levin, *Cold War University* (Madison: University of Wisconsin Press, 2013), 31–32.
3. "The Administration," *Time: The Weekly Newsmagazine* 90, no. 24 (December 15, 1967), 23–25.

CHAPTER 7
1. "Vietnam and Opposition at Home," Wisconsin Historical Society, www.wisconsinhistory.org/turningpoints/tp-040/?action=more_essay.

CHAPTER 8
1. Frank Newport, ed., *The Gallup Poll: Public Opinion 2012* (Blue Ridge Summit, PA: Roman and Littlefield, 2013), 316.

2. "The Nation: An Hour of Need," *Time: The Weekly Newsmagazine* 91, no. 15 (April 12, 1968).
3. United Press International, "Memphis Hunts Killer of Martin Luther King," *Wisconsin State Journal*, April 5, 1968.
4. United Press International, "Washington and Chicago Hardest Hit," *Wisconsin State Journal*, April 6, 1968.
5. Dennis Cassano, "Somber UW March Tells Reaction Here," *Wisconsin State Journal*, April 6, 1968.
6. Quoted in Matthew Levin, *Cold War University* (Madison: University of Wisconsin Press, 2013), 147.
7. Matthew Levin, *Cold War University* (Madison: University of Wisconsin Press, 2013), 143.

CHAPTER 9
1. "Men of the Year," *Time: The Weekly Newsmagazine* 93, no. 1 (January 3, 1969), 9–12.
2. University of Wisconsin–Madison, www.library.wisc.edu/archives/exhibits/campus-history-projects/protests-social-action-at-uw-madison-during-the-20th-century/1960-1969.
3. Ibid.
4. "Timeline: Major Events of the 1960s; 1967–1969," History Bibliographies, www.historybiblios.wordpress.com/the-1960s/timeline-1967-1969.
5. Raymond Merle, "Strike Continues, Despite Court Ban," *Wisconsin State Journal*, March 29, 1969.
6. Frank Newport, ed., *The Gallup Poll: Public Opinion 2012* (Blue Ridge Summit, PA: Roman and Littlefield, 2013), 316.
7. "Timeline: Major Events of the 1960s; 1967–1969."
8. "The War: Changing Atmosphere," *Time: The Weekly Newsmagazine* 94, no. 26 (December 26, 1969), 7–8.

CHAPTER 10
1. William Park, "President Nixon Imposes Wage and Price Controls," *The Econ Review*, www.econreview.com/events/wageprice1971b.htm.
2. University of Wisconsin–Madison, www.library.wisc.edu/archives/exhibits/campus-history-projects/protests-social-action-at-uw-madison-during-the-20th-century/1970-1979.
3. Ibid.
4. Ibid.

5. "The 1970 Postal Strike," *Pushing the Envelope: Smithsonian's National Postal Museum Blog*, March 17, 2010, http:// postalmuseumblog.si.edu/2010/03/the-1970-postal-strike.html.

6. "Madison and Earth Day Speeches," Earth Day Network, www.earthday.org/about/the-history-of-earth-day.

7. Ibid.

8. "The Kent State Shootings," Ohio History Connection, www.ohiohistorycentral.org/w/Kent_State_Shootings.

9. "Campus Report: The University of Wisconsin–Madison," *University News and Publications* 6, no. 8 (October 1, 1970).

10. Memo: Fred Harvey Harrington, University of Wisconsin Central Administration, October 1, 1970, vol. 13, no. 7.

CHAPTER 11

1. William Park, "President Nixon Imposes Wage and Price Controls," *The Econ Review*, www.econreview.com/events/wageprice1971b.htm.

2. "Top News Stories from 1972," InfoPlease, www.infoplease.com/year/1972.html.

3. "Vietnam War Timeline: 1971–1972," Vietnam Gear, www.vietnamgear.com/war1971.aspx.

4. "Enrollments 1888 to Present," Office of the Registrar, University of Wisconsin–Madison, https://registrar.wisc.edu/enrollments_1888_to_present.htm.

Acknowledgments

Several people helped with this book's development. My wife, Ruth, read and commented on the manuscript several times. As my readers have heard me say, "If my writing doesn't get past Ruth, it doesn't go anywhere."

I am forever indebted to the Wisconsin Historical Society Press, with Kathy Borkowski as director, for their commitment to publishing my work. And Kate Thompson, editor in chief, deserves far more credit than I am able to give for her tireless efforts to make my sometimes wandering prose readable.

About the Author

Jerry Apps has a PhD degree from the University of Wisconsin–Madison School of Education. He worked for the University of Wisconsin for thirty-eight years in varying roles, from county extension agent to tenured professor. From 1964 to 1974, he held joint appointments with UW–Madison and UW–Extension, serving as associate director for the Division of Program and Staff Development.

Apps edited the national *Journal of Extension* and served as commissioner for the American Council on Education in Washington, DC. He has been a Distinguished Visiting Professor at the University of Alaska and at the University of Alberta; a Landsdowne Scholar at the University of Victoria; and a consultant for the New York State Office of Higher Education, the province of Ontario, and other universities in the United States and Canada. Apps also served ten years in the US Army Reserves, reaching the rank of captain.

In addition to his many books on rural history, he has written eleven books on continuing and higher education. From 1989 to 1994, Apps was director of the National Center for Extension Leadership Development. He has received many awards for his writing, teaching, and leadership work in continuing and higher education. Today he is a rural historian and writer; he and his wife, Ruth, split their time between their home in Madison and their farm in central Wisconsin. Wisconsin Public Television has produced four hour-long documentaries featuring Jerry and his work.

Discover More Books by Jerry Apps

Limping through Life:
A Farm Boy's Polio Memoir

Never Curse the Rain:
A Farm Boy's Reflections on Water

Whispers and Shadows:
A Naturalist's Memoir

The Quiet Season:
Remembering Country Winters

Living a Country Year:
Wit and Wisdom from the Good Old Days

Every Farm Tells a Story:
A Tale of Farm Family Values

Roshara Journal:
Chronicling Four Seasons, Fifty Years,
and 120 Acres